The Handy Book
of Parish Law

WILLIAM ANDREWS HOLDSWORTH

CAMBRIDGE
UNIVERSITY PRESS

CAMBRIDGE UNIVERSITY PRESS

Cambridge, New York, Melbourne, Madrid, Cape Town, Singapore,
São Paolo, Delhi, Dubai, Tokyo, Mexico City

Published in the United States of America by Cambridge University Press, New York

www.cambridge.org
Information on this title: www.cambridge.org/9781108024839

© in this compilation Cambridge University Press 2010

This edition first published 1872
This digitally printed version 2010

ISBN 978-1-108-02483-9 Paperback

THE

HANDY BOOK

OF

PARISH LAW.

BY

W. A. HOLDSWORTH, Esq.,

OF GRAY'S INN, BARRISTER-AT-LAW,
AUTHOR OF "THE LAW OF LANDLORD AND TENANT," ETC.

THIRD EDITION.

LONDON:
GEORGE ROUTLEDGE AND SONS,
THE BROADWAY, LUDGATE.

LONDON :
PRINTED BY WOODFALL AND KINDER,
MILFORD LANE, STRAND, W.C.

CONTENTS.

PREFACE.

THE object of the following work is to present within a small compass a popular and practical statement of the most important portions of parochial law. Few subjects have a wider interest; for the parish is the unit of that great system of local self-government which is the foundation of English freedom. And although that self-government is now conducted to a considerable extent, in larger districts, through more complicated arrangements, and with a greater interference on the part of the Government of the country, than formerly, the ancient parochial organization is in many important respects untouched, which in almost every instance where this is not the case, the old is wisely incorporated with the new machinery. Notwithstanding all the innovations introduced by modern legislation, it is still the province of " parish law " to regulate our rights and duties in regard to the established church. It is by parish officers that the highways of the country are maintained and preserved. To them is committed the execution of recent acts for improving the sanitary condition of the country. They are still in some degree responsible for the preserva-

PREFACE.

tion of· the peace. Local taxation is almost entirely
levied through their intervention. And although,
under the New Poor Law, parishes have been combined into unions, it is by the separate parishes that
the administrators of the new system are elected;
and to these we have to recur when we investigate the
right of the poor to relief, their privilege (or disability)
of settlement, and their liability of removal. The
legislation relating to these and many other topics is
embraced in the general expression " parish law." It
is a wide field, which in the professional library em-
braces bulky volumes, and it is, therefore, with due
diffidence and a becoming sense of imperfection, that
we submit this slight attempt to place a mastery of
its salient features within the compass of a few hours'
reading.

2, CHURCHYARD COURT, TEMPLE.
October, 1st, 1859.

PREFACE TO THE THIRD EDITION.

SINCE the last edition of this work, many alterations
have been made in, and additions to, Parochial Law.
Provision has been made for the resignation of their
benefices by incumbents disabled from the performance
of their duties by age or infirmity. An act has been
passed with regard to the sequestration of the livings
of incumbents who have become insolvent. Church
rates have ceased to be levied compulsorily; while an
entirely new body, called Church Trustees, has been
called into existence, to assist members of the establishment in making provision for the repair of the
fabrics of their places of worship. The introduction
of Tramways has necessitated legislation conferring
upon the local authorities many powers and duties in
connection with this new means of communication.
Important changes have been effected in the various
branches of the Poor Law, extending not only to the
mode of rating certain classes of tenements, but to the
general administration of relief, and the treatment of
paupers. The "religious difficulty" in workhouses
has been dealt with in a very careful and elaborate
manner; superannuation allowances have been granted
to poor-law officers; and some amendments have been

made in the law relating to the election of boards of
guardians. In London, District Asylum boards have
been called into existence; and a considerable advance
has been made towards the equalization of the burthen
of pauperism throughout the metropolis. The law of
settlement and removal has undergone extensive modifications. The powers of the local authorities in
regard to sanitary matters have been increased. And
minor, but not unimportant changes, too numerous to
mention here, have been effected in almost every department of the law treated of in the following pages.
In the present edition, these changes, modifications,
and additions have been embodied. Several new
chapters have been inserted; and we venture to hope
that, in its revised form, our Handy-book will be
found a correct summary of Parish Law as it now
exists.

4, BRICK COURT, TEMPLE.
March, 1872.

HANDY BOOK OF PARISH LAW.

CHAPTER I.

OF THE PARISH AND PARISHIONERS.

THE parish is the integer both of our political and our ecclesiastical systems. But although in modern times it has been equally important in relation to either, there is no doubt that, in the first instance, it bore exclusive reference to the latter system. The earliest territorial divisions recognized by the church were, unquestionably, dioceses. The subsequent division of these into parishes was the result of the growth of population. When Christianity was struggling with surrounding heathenism, it is probable that the whole of the spiritual staff of a diocese was attached to the person of the bishop, and that its members were despatched by him, more as missionaries than as permanent ministers, into the different portions of his diocese. But as the numbers of believers increased, it became necessary that resident clergymen should be always at hand to administer to them the consolations of religion; and the natural result was, the division of the diocese into separate parishes, each with its own pastor. Moreover, the landlords, partly from motives of piety, and partly from a desire to strengthen the ties which bound their tenants to them, early began to

B

build churches upon their estates, and (with the sanction of the ecclesiastical authorities) to compel their dependants to pay their tithes to the support of these, instead of distributing them amongst the clergy of the diocese generally. The district whose tithes were thus appropriated to a particular church became a distinct parish. That parishes were, for the most part, thus formed, is clear from the fact that the boundaries of the oldest parishes are generally conterminous with those of one or more manors—probably originally belonging to the same lord. Considerable difference of opinion prevails amongst antiquaries as to the period at which the division of England into parishes took place. No doubt it was not a sudden, but a gradual process, extending over one, or perhaps two centuries. It appears, however, nearly certain that it was completed before the Norman Conquest, which occurred A.D. 1066. It must not, however, be supposed that the existing distribution of parishes ascends, in all cases, to that remote period. As population increased, the more extensive districts—particularly those embraced in the large towns—were divided and sub-divided, in order that their inhabitants might be brought more closely and immediately under clerical supervision. Besides those portions of the kingdom which thus became included in parishes, there were other lands which, either because they were in the hands of irreligious or careless owners, or were situate in forests or deserts,* or for other unsearchable reasons, were never united to any parish, and were, therefore, extra-parochial.

Although such places are still, in a certain sense,

* Blackstone's Commentaries, p. 114.

extra-parochial, they no longer enjoy the immunity
from local burthens which they formerly possessed.
For by the 20 Vict. c. 19, s. 1, it is enacted, that every
place entered separately in the report of the Registrar-
General on the Census of 1851, or which is there reported to be extra-parochial, and wherein no rate was
then levied for the poor, shall for all the purposes of
the assessment to the poor-rate, the relief of the poor,
the county, police, or borough rates, the burial of the
dead, the removal of nuisances, the registration of
parliamentary and municipal votes, and the registration of births and deaths, be deemed a parish for such
purposes, and shall be designated by the name assigned
to it in such report; and justices having jurisdiction
over such place, or the greater part thereof, shall
appoint overseers therein; and with respect to any
other place being, or reputed to be, extra-parochial, and
wherein no rate is levied for the relief of the poor, such
justices may appoint overseers of the poor. By sect. 4,
the quarter sessions or the recorder of a borough (if
situate in a borough subject to his jurisdiction) may
annex any extra-parochial place to an adjoining parish.
And then it was provided by the 29 & 30 Vict. c. 113 (the
Poor Law Amendment Act, 1866), that in all statutes,
except there shall be something inconsistent therewith, the word "parish" shall signify a place for which
a separate poor-rate is or can be made, or for which a
separate overseer is or can be appointed. By these
two Acts taken together, all extra-parochial places have
now been completely absorbed into the parochial system
of the country, at any rate, in so far as relates to the
administration of the poor laws.

The boundaries of parishes generally depend upon ancient and immemorial custom. In most parishes in the country "perambulations" are made in Rogation week, for the purpose of keeping up the memory of those boundaries; and it is well established that parishioners are entitled to go over any man's land in their perambulations. But an entry into a particular house cannot be justified, or a custom to that effect supported, unless the house stands on the boundary-line, and it is necessary to enter it for the purpose of the perambulation.

When a dispute arises with respect to the boundaries of a parish, the proper mode to decide the question is, in general, by an action in one of the courts of common law. *For the purposes of rating, indeed,* the justices of the peace in sessions may decide * in which of two neighbouring parishes improved wastes and drained and improved marsh-lands lie. Under the General Enclosure Act (8 & 9 Vict. c. 118, s. 39), the enclosure commissioners may settle the boundaries of any parish or manor in which land is to be enclosed. And a similar power is given to the tithe commissioners (1 Vict. c. 69, s. 2), when the tithes of any parish or district are to be commuted. They can, however, only exercise it at the request of two-thirds in value of the owners of lands therein, signified in writing under their hands, or the hands of their agents, and signed at a parochial meeting called for the purpose.

We have hitherto spoken of "parishes" which bear that character both for *civil* and for *ecclesiastical* purposes. There is, however, a class of parishes generally

* Under the 17 Geo. II. c. 37.

called "new parishes," which has reference only to the latter. Under certain acts of parliament,* the ecclesiastical commissioners may, by an order in council, divide any parish into two or more separate parishes for all ecclesiastical purposes, and fix the respective proportion of tithes, glebe lands, and other endowments which are to remain to each. To this division the consent of the patron of the living, and of the bishop of the diocese, is requisite; and it can only take effect (except with the consent of the incumbent) at the next vacancy in the living. The incumbent of every new parish thus formed has the exclusive cure of souls within it, and the exclusive right of performing all ecclesiastical offices within its limits for the resident inhabitants thereof, who are thenceforth, for all ecclesiastical purposes, parishioners thereof.

We have just used the word parishioners. It may be as well to define its legal meaning. It includes "not only inhabitants of the parish, but persons who are occupiers of lands, who pay the several rates and duties, although they are not resident nor do contribute to the ornaments of the church."

"Inhabitants" includes all "housekeepers, though not rated to the poor, and also all persons who are not housekeepers; as, for instance, those who have gained a settlement, and by that means become inhabitants." Persons staying casually for a few weeks in a parish do not come under either of the terms "parishioner" or "inhabitant."

* 6 & 7 Vict. c. 37; 7 & 8 Vict. c. 94; and 19 & 20 Vict c. 104.

CHAPTER II.

OF THE PARISH CHURCH AND CHURCHYARD.

THE freehold of the body or nave of the church is in the parson, and if any injury is done to it, he is the proper person to bring an action for damages. The "aisles" of the church frequently belong, either wholly or in part, to private families or individuals, or rather to particular estates within the parish, the owners of which, it is supposed, originally erected the aisle for the accommodation of themselves or their household. In support of such a claim, it is necessary not only that the right should have existed immemorially, but that the owners of the property, in respect of which it is claimed, should have repaired this part of the church from time to time. The freehold of the "chancel" is in the rector, who is charged with the responsibility of repairing it.

By the general law and of common right, all the pews in a parish church are the common property of the parish; they are for the use, in common, of the parishioners, who are all entitled to be seated orderly and conveniently, so as best to provide for the accommodation of all. They have indeed a claim to be seated according to their rank and station, but the churchwardens, who in this respect act as the officers of the bishop of the diocese, and subject to his control, are not, in providing for this, to overlook the claims of all the parishioners to be seated, if sittings

can be afforded them.   Accordingly, they are bound, in
particular, not to accommodate the higher classes beyond their real wants, to the exclusion of their poorer
neighbours, who are equally entitled to accommodation
with the rest, though they are not entitled to equal
accommodation ; supposing the seats not to be all
equally convenient.   And every parishioner has a right
to a seat in the church without any payment, either
for the purchase or as rent for the same ; and if necessary, occupiers of pews, who are not parishioners (having no prescriptive right therein), may be put out by
the churchwardens, to enable them to seat parishioners.
And although such occupier has purchased the seat,
and it was erected under a "faculty," * containing a
clause permitting the party erecting the same to sell
it, this will not avail against the common-law right
of parishioners, for such permission in the faculty is
illegal.

An individual may, however, acquire such an exclusive
right to a pew, that neither the churchwardens nor
the bishop of the diocese can oust him.   This arises
either from a "faculty" having been issued by a
bishop of the diocese, granting the pew to him, or to his
ancestors and their heirs, or to the owners of property
now held by him in the parish.   A long-continued enjoy-
ment and repair of a pew by a man, his ancestors, or the
holders of particular land, whether within or without
the parish, will be held to presuppose a "faculty," and
will confer a prescriptive right to the pew in question.

Whenever it is determined to pull down or enlarge
the church, or to make a new distribution of the

* *i.e.* A permission or grant from the bishop.

pews and sittings in the church, the consent of the
inhabitants, in vestry assembled, should be first obtained.   This having been done, the churchwardens
should obtain a faculty from the bishop,* empowering
them to make the necessary alterations, and a commission is then issued to certain clergymen and laymen,
authorizing them to allot the sittings.   This they are
generally directed to do in the following order : 1st, to
those who had, before the issuing of the commission,
seats by faculty or prescription, who are to have others
allotted to them as near as may be to the site of their
former seats ; 2nd, to those who have contributed by
their subscriptions to the building, enlargement, or
repairs, or have actually occupied seats, though not
by faculty or prescription, who are to have sittings
according to the amount of their subscription, their
quality, and the number of their families, but only so
long as they continue to abide in the parish, and habi-
tually resort to church ; 3rd, to the rest of the inhabitants according to their station and requirements, and
on the same tenure.

If any person erects any pew or seat in a church
without a licence from the bishop, or without the con-

* One of the churchwardens of a parish, accompanied by
another parishioner, acting upon a resolution of the vestry,
but against the expressed prohibition of the rector, and without
any lawful authority from the bishop of the diocese, broke
open with a crowbar the principal door of the parish church,
and with the assistance of some workmen proceeded to alter
the position of the pulpit, and to pull down and re-arrange
certain of the seats within the church.   Held, that all who
took part in these proceedings had been guilty of a grave
ecclesiastical offence. *Dewdney* v. *Good*, 7 Jurist, N.S., 637.

sent of the minister or churchwardens, or in an incon-
venient place, or if he make the sides too high, it may
be pulled down by order from the bishop or his archdeacon, or by the churchwardens, or by the consent
of the parson ; but if any presume, without such
authority, to cut or pull down any seat annexed to the
church, the parson may have an action of trespass
against the misdoer.

Under one of the acts to which we have referred
for forming new parishes, it is provided, that if sufficient funds cannot otherwise be provided for the endow-
ment of the church of such a parish, annual rents
may (with the sanction of the ecclesiastical commissioners and of the bishop of the diocese) be taken for the
pews or sittings.   But half, at, least, of the sittings
must still be free, and it must be proved to the satisfaction of the commissioners that such seats are as
advantageously situated as those for which a rent is
taken.

With respect to the furnishing of the parish church,
it is laid down that the parish is bound to provide
everything which is necessary for the due and orderly
celebration of the services of the church and the administration of the sacraments.   Such are the following :—a communion-table, a pulpit, a reading-desk, a
font, a chest for alms, a chalice, wine, bread, &c., a
bible, prayer-book, and book of homilies ; bells, ropes,
and a bier for the dead; a table of the prohibited de-
grees of marriage, and another of the ten command-
ments.

Monuments, tomb-stones, &c., cannot be erected in
a church or churchyard without the consent of the

parson and churchwardens; and also, strictly speaking, of the bishop of the diocese, whose jurisdiction in this matter is, however, rarely appealed to. He may, indeed, remove them if they are put up without his consent. After monuments have been erected they may be repaired; and the churchwardens are bound to consent to this.

If there be no custom that the parish or the owner of a particular estate should repair the chancel of the church, the responsibility of doing so rests at common law with the parson;* while the parishioners are charged with the duty of repairing the church. Since the abolition of compulsory church rates it is, however, a duty the fulfilment of which there is no means of enforcing. If it be necessary to enlarge the church, or to pull it down and rebuild it, the consent of a majority of the parishioners declared at a meeting duly summoned, and upon proper notice, must be obtained. The churchwardens must also take care to obtain the previous concurrence of the parish to a rate for the purpose—they cannot, after the alterations are made, call upon the parish to reimburse them.

The freehold of a church being in the incumbent, the custody of the key lawfully belongs to him. One consequence of this is, that unless he consents, the parishioners cannot, except on the occasion of divine worship, procure the ringing of the church bells.

By 24 & 25 Vict. c. 97, s. 1, and the 27 & 28 Vict. c. 47, any person unlawfully and maliciously setting

---

* In London there is a custom for the parishioners to repair the chancel as well as the nave.

fire to any church, chapel, meeting-house, or other
place of divine worship, shall be guilty of felony, and
shall be liable to be kept in penal servitude for life, or
for any term not less than five years, or to be imprisoned for any term not exceeding two years, with
or without hard labour, and with or without solitary
confinement; and if a male under the age of sixteen
years, with or without whipping.* By the 24 & 25
Vict. c. 97, s. 39, it is made a misdemeanour to maliciously destroy or damage any picture, statue, monu-
ment or other memorial of the dead, painted glass, or
other ornament or work of art in any church, chapel,
meeting-house, or other place of divine worship, or in
any church or burial-ground. And the 7 & 8 Geo. 4,
c. 30, s. 8, as amended by the 4 & 5 Vict. c. 56, s. 2,
enacts, that persons riotously assembled and demolish-
ing, or beginning to demolish, any place of worship
(as above), are guilty of felony, and liable to transportation for not less than seven years, or imprisonment, with or without hard labour, for not more than
three years. By the 7 & 8 Geo. 4, c. 31, if any church
or chapel, or any chapel for the religious worship of
persons dissenting from the united church of England
and Ireland, shall be feloniously demolished, wholly or
in part, by persons riotously or tumultuously assembled
together, the inhabitants of the hundred, or district in
the nature of a hundred, shall be liable to compensate
the persons damnified by the offence. By sect. 8,

* With respect to the punishment for breaking into or out
of a church, chapel, or meeting-house, or committing a felony
therein, see 24 & 25 Vict. c. 96, s. 50 & 51, and the 27 & 28
Vict. c. 47.

where the damage does not exceed £30, the party damnified is not to proceed by action, but shall give a written notice of his claim for compensation within seven days to the high constable, who shall exhibit it within seven days to two justices, and they shall, within not less than thirty days, appoint a special petty session for hearing and determining such claim. Every action, by sect. 11, shall be brought in the name of the rector, vicar, or curate, or, if there be none, in the names of the church or chapel wardens, or in the name of any person in whom the property of the chapel is vested.

At common law, the parishioners are bound to repair the fences of the churchyard, although custom may in particular cases throw the obligation upon either the parson or the owners of particular estates. But the parishioners have no power to cut down trees, or mow the grass of the churchyard, without the consent of the parson, to whom they belong. He can, however, only cut down the trees (unless they are decayed) for the repair of the church or the parsonage-house. And although the freehold of the churchyard—as of the church—is in the parson, tombstones therein set up belong to those who erected them.

If an existing churchyard is full, or is inadequate to meet the wants of the parish, the ecclesiastical commissioners may (under 59 Geo. 3, c. 134, s. 36) call upon the churchwardens to summon a meeting of the parishioners in vestry assembled, to take all necessary measures (including the levy of a rate) for enlarging such existing churchyard, or making an additional one. And the said commissioners are empowered to authorize any parish to purchase the necessary land, levy the requisite rates, and do other acts for the purpose of providing such additional churchyard accommodation. Whenever any land is added to a consecrated churchyard, by the gift of any person, whether resident or not, in the parish or ecclesiastical district in which such churchyard is situated, such giver may reserve the exclusive rights in perpetuity of burial and of placing monuments and gravestones in a part of the land so added not exceeding 50 square yards, or a sixth of the whole.*

On the other hand (under the 15 & 16 Vict. c. 85, extended by 16 & 17 Vict. c. 134, and amended by the 18 & 19 Vict. c. 128), the Queen in council, on the representation of a secretary of state, that sanitary considerations require the discontinuance of burial in any churchyard, or other burial-ground in London, or any other populous place, may order burials to be so discontinued, either wholly or under certain conditions, after a day to be fixed.† Persons burying, or assisting to bury, or the keepers of any such ground permitting interments to take place there, after that day, are guilty of a misdemeanor ; and any

* 30 & 31 Vict. c. 133, s. 7.

† No such order in council is to extend to any burial-ground of Quakers or Jews, used solely for the burial of such people or persons, unless the same be expressly mentioned in the order ; and nothing in the act is to prevent the burial in any such burial-ground, in which interment is not required to be discontinued, of such people or persons. And no such order in council is to extend to any non-parochial burial-ground, being the property of a private person, unless expressly mentioned in the order.

person knowingly and wilfully burying, or assisting in such burial, is further subject to a penalty not exceeding £10, summarily recoverable on application to two justices of the peace. The secretary of state may permit persons who had, previously to the issue of the order in council, a right under any faculty legally granted, or by usage or otherwise, to bury in vaults in or under such ground, churchyard, or burial-ground, to continue the exercise of that right, upon being satisfied that no injury to the public health will accrue. Such churchyard, or burial-ground, is to be maintained out of the poor-rates, in decent order by the churchwardens or burial-board, as the case may be.

The above statutes contain various provisions applicable to the provision of new burial-grounds in lieu of such as have been closed by order of the secretary of state, or appear to be insufficient or injurious to health. The churchwardens (or other persons whose duty it is to summon meetings of the parish vestry), upon the requisition in writing of ten or more ratepayers of any parish in which the places of burial appear to such ratepayers insufficient or dangerous to health (whether any order in council in relation to such parish has or has not been made), or at their own discretion, without requisition in any parish in which no burial-board has been appointed, are to summon a special meeting of the vestry to determine whether a burial-ground shall be provided for the parish. Seven days' notice of such meeting is to be given, and if it is then determined to provide a new burial-ground, a copy of the resolution or resolutions to that effect is to be sent to the secretary of state for the home depart-

ment.   And in order to carry out such resolution or
resolutions, the vestry are to appoint a burial-board,
consisting of not less than three nor more than nine
ratepayers of the parish, one-third of whom are to go
out of office yearly at a time fixed by the vestry.
Parishes may concur (15 & 16 Vict. c. 85, s. 23) in
providing a common burial-ground, and may agree as
to the proportion in which the expenses shall be borne
by the several parishes; and according and subject to
such terms the several boards are to act as a joint board
for all the parishes, and to have joint officers.   The
burial-board is forthwith to purchase land * and take
other necessary steps for the provision of a burial-
ground, or it may contract with a cemetery company
for the interment in their ground of persons who
would have had rights of burial in the burial-
grounds of the parish.   Unless the vestry *unanimously*
decide that the whole of the new burial-ground is to
be consecrated, it must be divided into consecrated
and unconsecrated parts in such proportions, and the
unconsecrated part allotted in such manner and in
such portions, as sanctioned by the secretary of state;
and when a burial-board builds on any burial-ground
a chapel for the performance of the burial-service of
the church, they must also (unless three-fourths of the
vestry decide that this is unnecessary) build on the
unconsecrated part chapel accommodation for the performance of burial-service by persons not being members of the church.   The management of the new

* No new burial-ground can be made within 100 yards of
any dwelling-house, without the consent in writing of the
owner, lessee, or occupier thereof.

burial-ground is vested in the burial-boards, whose expenses in carrying the act into execution are to be defrayed out of the poor rate, by borrowing money, or by the income arising from the burial-ground. Subject to certain fees and payments fixed by the acts to which we have referred, the board are to fix all fees for interments, &c., and as soon as the new burial-ground is consecrated it is to be deemed the burial-ground for the parish or united parishes for which it is provided, and the incumbent or minister and the clerk and sexton thereof are to perform the same duties, and have the same rights and authorities for the performance of religious service, in the burial there of the remains of parishioners and others, and shall be entitled to receive the same fees as heretofore ; and the parishioners of such parish or parishes are to have in the new ground the same rights of sepulture as they had in their old churchyard or burial-ground.

In boroughs, town councils may, on their own petition, be appointed, by order of the Queen in council, the burial-boards of such boroughs ; and in that case all the powers of such boards are vested in them ; while their acts require no confirmation by the vestry. And where the district of any local board of health established under the Public Health Act, or of any commissioners elected by the ratepayers, and acting under any local act for the improvement of any town, parish, or borough, is coextensive with the district for which it is proposed to provide a burial-ground (and no burial-board has been appointed), Her Majesty in council may, upon the petition of such local board, or of such board of commissioners, appoint them to be the burial-board for their own district. The expenses of such local board may be paid out of the general district rate or by a separate rate.

Every parishioner has, and always had, a right to be buried in the churchyard or burial-ground of his parish. And the Court of Queen's Bench will issue a mandamus to compel a clergyman to inter the body of a parishioner. Also by the 48 Geo. III. c. 75, s. 1, the churchwardens and overseers in any parish in which a dead body is cast on shore from the sea, are to bury it in the parish churchyard or burial-ground, the expenses being reimbursed to them out of the county rate on an order from a justice of the peace.

Every householder in whose house a corpse lies is bound by the common law to have it decently interred, and a parent must, if he is able, provide Christian burial for the body of his child. The guardians, or, where there are no guardians, the over-seers of the poor, may bury the body of any poor person which may be in their parish or union, and charge the expenses to any parish under their control, to which such person may have been chargeable, or in which he may have died, or otherwise in which such body may be.

And all persons are entitled to be buried by the parson of the parish, or the officiating clergyman at the burial-ground, with the rites of the church of England, except persons excommunicated by an ecclesiastical court; or who are unbaptized, or who have committed suicide. With respect to the two latter classes, we should observe that baptism by a dissent-

c

ing minister or a layman * is quite sufficient to entitle
a person to Christian burial by a clergyman of the
Church of England; and that to disentitle to such
Christian burial, the suicide must have been committed
when the person destroying himself was sane.

The fees payable for burial in churchyards are subject to the sanction of the bishop. The proportion in
which they are divided between the churchwardens and
the parson depends upon the usage of each parish. As
to the fees chargeable in respect of interment in the
new burial-grounds, we have already seen that the
burial-boards are entitled (under some reservations) to
fix them.

CHAPTER III.

OF THE PARSON AND CLERGYMEN OF THE PARISH, AND CHURCH SERVICES.

WE shall enter but very cursorily into the subjects
embraced under this head; for, in truth, they belong
rather to ecclesiastical than to parish law, in the proper
sense of the term; while they involve so many and

* The law on this point is settled by the case of *Escott* v.
Mastin, 4 Moore P. C. C. 104. The marginal note to this case
is, "A child baptized with water *in the name of the Trinity* by
a layman (a Wesleyan methodist), not authorized to administer
the rite of baptism. Held not to be 'unbaptized' within
the meaning of the rubric for the burial of the dead in the
Common Prayer Book as incorporated into the Uniformity
Act, 13 & 14 Car. II. c. 4." It would appear from this case
that the baptism, to be valid, must be *in the name of the
Trinity.*

such complicated considerations, that any attempt to popularize them would be productive of harm rather than good. We shall, therefore, content ourselves with adverting to a few practical points, which are of chief interest to the parishioners. One of them is the performance of service. By the 58th Geo. III. c. 45, s. 65, the bishop may direct a third service to be performed, in given circumstances, in any church or chapel of his diocese. And he may also (1 & 2 Vict. c. 106, s. 80) require an incumbent to perform two full services, including a sermon or lecture on every Sunday, during the whole or part of the year, in any benefice of whatever value; and also in the church or chapel of every parish or chapelry where a benefice is composed of two or more parishes or chapelries, if the annual income derived by the incumbent from that parish or chapelry is £150, and its population 400.

Clergymen are protected from arrest on civil process while performing or going to or returning from the performance of divine service; and they are also exempted from the payment of turnpike tolls while engaged in their parish in the performance of parochial duties. On the other hand, they are disqualified from being members of parliament; councillors or aldermen of any borough; sheriffs, constables, or overseers of the poor. They are exempt from serving as parish officers, or upon juries. They are not allowed to trade; nor, without permission from the bishop, to farm more than eighty acres of land. If they are guilty of immorality, irregularity in the discharge of their duties, or preaching contrary to the articles of the church, they are liable to be punished

c 2

by admonition, suspension from the fulfilment of their sacred office, degradation or deprivation, *i. e.* the loss of their holy orders or of their benefice. They are proceeded against under the Church Discipline Act (3 & 4 Vict. c. 86). Under this act, if charges are made against them, the bishop, in the first instance, issues a commission to inquire whether there is a *primâ facie* case for further proceedings. If the report is in the affirmative, and the clergyman still denies the charge, the cause is heard by the bishop, assisted by assessors, two legal and one clerical. From their sentence there is an appeal to the judge of the province; *i. e.* if in the province of Canterbury, to the Arches Court in London; and if in the province of York, to a similar tribunal at York.

If a clergyman is insolvent, or unable to pay his debts, the bishop will grant a " sequestration " of the living; *i. e.* he will authorize certain persons to receive the profits of the living, and apply them to the payment of the insolvent's debts. The law upon this point is now regulated by an act passed in the year 1871 (the 34 & 35 Vict. c. 45, or the Sequestration Act, 1871). By this it is enacted, that where, after the 31st day of August, 1871, under a judgment recovered against the incumbent of a benefice, or under the bankruptcy of such incumbent, a sequestration issues and remains in force for a period of six months, the bishop of the diocese shall, from and after the expiration of such period of six months, and as long as the sequestration remains in force, take order for the due performance of the services of the church of the benefice; and shall have power to appoint and license for this purpose such curate or curates, with such stipends as he thinks fit. The stipend or stipends payable to the curates must not, however, exceed in the whole the following sums, that is to say:—

If the population shall not exceed 500, the sum of £200 yearly.

If the population shall exceed 500, but not 1,000, the sum of £300 yearly.

If the population shall exceed 1,000, but not 3,000, the sum of £500 pounds yearly.

If the population shall exceed 3,000, the sum of £600 yearly.

Provided also, that such stipend or stipends shall not exceed in the whole two-thirds of the annual value of the benefice.

Every stipend assigned under this act is (by sect. 3) to be paid by the sequestrator out of moneys coming to his hands under the sequestration, as long as the sequestration is in force, in priority to all sums payable by virtue of the judgment or the bankruptcy under which the sequestration issues, but not in priority of liabilities in respect of charges on the benefice.

In case any sequestration remains in force for more than six months, the bishop, if it appears to him that scandal or inconvenience is likely to arise from the incumbent continuing to perform the services of the church while the sequestration remains in force, may, from and after the expiration of such period, inhibit him from performing any services of the church within the diocese as long as the sequestration

remains in force; and the bishop may at any time
withdraw such inhibition.*

While any sequestration subsists, the incumbent is
absolutely disabled from presenting or nominating to
any benefice then vacant, of which he may be patron
in right of the benefice under sequestration; and the
right of presentation or nomination to such vacant
benefice will be exercised by the bishop of the diocese
in which the benefice is locally situate.†

During the continuance of any sequestration, it is
not lawful for the incumbent of the benefice under
sequestration to accept, or be instituted, or licensed,
to any other benefice or preferment, the acceptance of,
or institution, or licensing to which would avoid or
vacate the benefice so under sequestration, unless with
the consent, in writing, of the bishop of the diocese
and the sequestrator. ‡

One of the most important points in connection with
this part of our subject is, the law as to the residence
of the clergyman in his benefice. That is now regulated by the 1 & 2 Vict. c. 106, by the thirty-second
section of which, " if any spiritual person, holding a
benefice, shall absent himself from it, or from the house
of residence, for any period exceeding three months
together, or to be accounted at several times, in one
year, he is to forfeit—if the absence exceed three,
but not six months, one-third; if it exceed six, but not
eight months, one-half; if it exceed eight months, two-
thirds; if for the whole year, three-fourths of the
annual value, unless he has such licence or exemption
as is by the act allowed, or unless he be resident at

* Sec. 5.   † Sec. 6.   ‡ Sec. 7.

some other benefice of which he may be possessed."
Licences for non-residence may be granted by the
bishop for the following causes :—

1. On account of incapacity of mind or body.
2. For six months—and only to be renewed with
   the allowance of the archbishop, under his
   hand—on account of the dangerous illness of
   wife or child, making part of his family and
   residing with him.
3. On account of there being no house of residence,
   or the house being unfit for residence, such un-
   fitness not being caused by the neglect or misconduct of the petitioner.
4. [This applies merely to non-residence in the parsonage-house.] On account of occupying, in
   the same parish, a mansion whereof he is owner,
   he at the same time keeping the house of residence in good repair.*

A non-resident incumbent is bound to provide a
curate, or curates, to perform his duties during his
absence, and their stipends are fixed by the act to
which we have just referred. If he fails to do so, the
bishop may appoint. Indeed, if the annual value of a
benefice, of which the incumbent was not in possession
at the time of the passing of the act (14th August,
1838), exceed £500, and the population amounts to
3,000, or if there be a second church or chapel two
miles distant from the mother church, with a hamlet
or district containing 400 persons, the bishop may
require the holder of such benefice, *though resident
and performing duty,* to appoint and pay a curate. If

* Steer's Parish Law, by Hodgson, p. 106.

the population exceed 2,000, and the incumbent (having become so since July 20, 1813) is non-resident, the bishop may require him to nominate two curates.

If an incumbent do not reside upon his living and perform duty there, the bishop is to appoint a curate, or curates. And the scale of payment to the curates of such non-resident incumbents as have acquired their living since July 20, 1813, is as follows :—

In no case less than £80, or the annual value if less than £80.

If the population amounts to 300, £100, or the annual value if less than £100.

If the population amounts to 500, £120, or the annual value if less than £120.

If the population amounts to 750, £135, or the annual value if less than £135.

If the population amounts to 1,000, £150, or the annual value if less than £150.

If the annual value exceed £400, and the curate be resident and have no other cure, the bishop may assign £100 as a stipend, though the population be not 300; and if it be 500, may add £50 to the stipend required by the act.

And it is by the same act expressly declared that any agreement by which a curate shall bind himself to accept less than his legal stipend, shall be utterly null and void.

There was, until recently, no means of making a provision for clergymen who might be incapacitated by age or illness from the performance of the duties of their benefices. If they resigned their livings they must do so without pension or allowance of any kind; and the result of course was, that instances of resignation were rare indeed. The law was placed upon a more rational footing by the "Incumbent's Resignation Act, 1871" (34 & 35 Vict. c. 44), which will probably have a material effect in improving and maintaining the efficiency of the parochial clergy. We shall therefore summarize its more important provisions, remarking at the outset, that it can, as will be seen, only be put in force by the incumbent. His resignation, if it takes place, must be his own voluntary act. We still require some means by which the parishioners can compel the resignation of an incumbent who can no longer perform his duties.

On a representation being made to the bishop in the form contained in the act, by the incumbent of any benefice (provided he has been the incumbent of such benefice for seven years continuously) that he desires, on the ground of being incapacitated by permanent mental or bodily infirmity from the due performance of his duties, to retire from his benefice, the bishop may cause a commission to be issued to five persons,*

* One of the five Commissioners must be the archdeacon of an archdeaconry, or the rural dean of a rural deanery of the diocese wherein the benefice is situate, as the bishop may determine; another an incumbent of the same diocese, nominated by the incumbent wishing to retire; another an incumbent of the same diocese, nominated by the bishop; another a magistrate being in the commission of the peace for the county wherein the benefice is situate, and a member of the Established Church of England, nominated by the person who has presided as chairman of the last preceding quarter sessions for the county or division of the county, or if there be no such person, then by the lord lieutenant of the county; and the remaining Commissioner must be nominated by the patron, or,

authorizing and requiring them to inquire into and report to him upon the truth of the ground alleged, and upon the expediency of the resignation of the incumbent. If the commissioners certify the resignation to be expedient, and the patron shall in writing have consented, or shall not within one calendar month thereafter in writing refuse his consent thereto, the bishop will proceed as we shall presently mention; but if the patron refuses his consent, the return to the commission must be laid before the archbishop of the province, who is, within one calendar month, to give his decision in writing whether such resignation shall or shall not be accepted, which decision shall be final. If the patron has declared his consent, or has not refused it, or if the archbishop decides that the resignation ought to be accepted, the bishop will cause a declaration to be prepared, inserting therein the amount of pension so allowed out of the revenues of the benefice to the retiring incumbent, and the day, not being less than one month after the date of the declaration, when the incumbency shall be void and the pension shall commence; the times of payment not being oftener than twice a year.

The pension so allowed is to be a charge upon the revenues of the benefice, and be recoverable as a debt at law or in equity from the incumbent of the said benefice by the retired clerk, his executors, administrators, or assigns, but such pension is not to be transferable at law or in equity.

in the case of alternate patronage, jointly by both or all of the patrons; or in case of difference, by the patron entitled to the next presentation.

The declaration of the bishop having been filed in the diocesan registry, the benefice will, *ipso facto,* be vacant on the day fixed in such declaration, and the patron will be entitled to present a clerk for the same, just as if it had been vacated by the death of the incumbent; and the clerk who is collated, instituted, or licensed thereto, will be entitled to the revenues, subject to the payment to the retired clerk of such sum as may be allowed to him as pension. The new incumbent will have the same right and claim in respect of dilapidations as if the benefice had been vacated by the death of the previous incumbent thereof.

It is in no case lawful to assign the house of residence of the incumbent as any part or the whole of the pension for a retired clerk; but such house of residence must in all cases belong to and be enjoyed by the incumbent of the benefice as if the benefice were free from all claim by a retired clerk.

The right of a retired clerk to the pension assigned to him will cease upon the enrolment of any deed of relinquishment by him, under the 33 & 34 Vict. c. 91, or on and after the day on which he is admitted to another benefice. And in the event of his undertaking clerical duties elsewhere than within the benefice from which he retired, the incumbent of the benefice may bring the fact to the notice of the bishop. If his lordship be satisfied that the retired clerk is or has been undertaking such clerical duties and receiving a remuneration for the same, he may (subject to an appeal to the archbishop) determine whether the pension payable to him shall cease, or be diminished in any and what proportion, or for any and what period.

The right of resignation and of doing any act leading to, connected with, or consequent on such resignation by this act given to an incumbent, may, if the
incumbent be a lunatic found such by inquisition, be
exercised in his name and on his behalf by the committee of his estate.

There can, we think, be no doubt that this act will
greatly conduce to the efficiency of the church.

THE RITES AND SACRAMENTS OF THE CHURCH.

Except in cases of necessity, when they may be
baptized at home, children, it is said, should be baptized in the church of the parish in which they were
born. But by the 60th canon, " if the acting minister,
being duly informed of the weakness and danger of
death of any infant unbaptized in the parish, and being
thereupon desired to go to its residence to baptize
it, shall either refuse or so defer the time that it dieth
unbaptized through his fault, he shall be suspended
for three months; and before his restitution shall ac-
knowledge his fault, and promise before his Ordinary
that he will not wittingly incur the like again."   No
fee is due of common right for christening a child, but
one may be payable by custom.

The principal points to be noticed in reference to the
administration of the Lord's supper are the following :
—The minister is to give notice on the Sunday, or on
some holiday immediately preceding, and those who
intend to be partakers shall signify their intention
some time the day before the communion.   But if
there be not a convenient number to communicate

there shall be no celebration; and there must be four, or three at the least even when the parish contains no more than twenty persons qualified to receive the communion. In all churches, convenient and decent communion-tables * being provided, they must be kept in a seemly condition, covered in time of divine service with a carpet of silk or other decent stuff; and at the time of ministration they should be covered with a fair linen cloth. And it is forbidden to administer the holy communion in private houses except in times of necessity to the dangerously sick and impotent. The churchwardens are to provide a sufficient quantity of fine white bread, and of good wholesome wine, with the advice of the minister. And if any remain unconsecrated the curate shall have it to his own use; but the surplus of that which is consecrated shall be eaten and drunken after the blessing in the church by the priest, and such communicants as he shall then call unto him (*Rubric to Communion Service*). By canon 27, no minister when he celebrates the communion shall wittingly administer the same to any but to such as kneel.†

The law with respect to the solemnization of marriages will be found . n the statutes 4 Geo. 4, c. 76, and the 6 &   Wm. 4, c. 85; and, as the subject is one which, if ntered upon at all, would require to be dealt with at considerable length, while it hardly comes under what is known as "parish law," we must refer our readers to the acts in question, or to treatises

---

* A stone altar fixed in the floor, and not movable, is not a communion-table.—*Falkner* v. *Litchfield*, 9 Jurist, 234.

† Steer's Parish Law, by Hodgson, p. 153.

within whose scope it more properly falls. It may, however, be useful to say a word or two here upon the subject of the fees payable upon marriages in a parish church, more especially as the law on this subject is in a rather confused and anomalous state. It is laid down by all the authorities, that "no fee whatever is due by common right (*i. e.* by common law) for performing the marriage ceremony." On the other hand, fees are payable by *ancient custom* in most parishes—the amount of course varying in each parish. That being the state of the law, it is impossible to say, without knowing what is the custom in the parish, whether in any given case a person is liable to pay any, and if so, what fees in respect of a marriage. It is, however, still an open question, whether the incumbent can refuse to perform the marriage until the fees are paid, or whether he is not bound to perform the ceremony first, and then take steps to recover the fees. It is also doubtful whether he can sue in any but the Ecclesiastical Court. And it is certain that if the custom can be shown to have originated since the time of Richard I. (in considering which question, the court will take into consideration the amount demanded, and the probability that it could have been paid in the twelfth century) it will be declared invalid. Such being the state of the law, it is obvious that most persons will avoid litigation by paying a demand which can hardly exceed a few shillings. If, indeed, a clergyman should ask 13*s.* or more as his own fee and that of the church, payment may be safely refused on the authority of *Bryant* v. *Foot*, 36 L. J., Q. B. 65. Indeed, it is evident, from the reasoning of the judges who decided this case, that they would have pronounced against a custom for a considerably smaller amount. Fees arc also payable by custom for the publishing of banns.

CHAPTER IV.

OF THE CHURCHWARDENS.

THE churchwardens are the guardians or keepers of the church, and the representatives of the body of the church. But although they have a right of access to the church at proper seasons, they are not entitled to the custody of the keys. They must be ratepayers and householders in the parish, and are, for some purposes, a kind of corporation, being enabled, as churchwardens, to have property, in goods and chattels, on behalf of the parishioners, and to bring actions for them. One churchwarden cannot singly dispose of the goods of the parish, nor even can both, without the consent of the parishioners. In addition to their ecclesiastical office, they are *ex officio* overseers in parishes maintaining their own poor : * and they are also *ex officio* members of a select vestry.

It is the usual, indeed almost invariable, practice, to have two churchwardens ; but a custom that there shall be only one in a particular parish is good.

The parishioners may, speaking generally, elect any householders, being also ratepayers, that they choose ; but it has been laid down, in a case of great authority,

* And by the 29 & 30 Vict. c. 113, s. 10, the same person may hold jointly the offices of churchwarden and overseer in any parish.

that if the parish returned persons utterly unqualified
for the office (for instance, a Papist, a Jew, a child, or
a person convicted of felony), the bishop of the diocese
would be entitled and bound to annul the election.
But the poverty of a churchwarden, however extreme,
is no objection to his election.

The following persons are exempted by various acts
of parliament from serving the office:—Peers, members of parliament, clergymen, Roman Catholic priests,
dissenting ministers, physicians, and surgeons being
freemen of the city of London ; apothecaries, having
served seven years; persons living out of the parish
though occupying land within it for purposes other
than those of trade;* sergeants, corporals, drummers,
and privates of militia; commissioners and officers of
excise and customs.   Quakers, also, will not be compelled to serve.

By the Toleration Act (1 Wm. and Mary, c. 18,
s. 7), it is also provided that if any person dissenting
from the church of England be appointed to the office
of churchwarden, or any other parochial office, and
scruple to take the oaths, &c., he may execute the
same by a sufficient deputy, to be approved in such
manner as the officer himself should by law have been
allowed and approved; and similar provisions with
respect to Roman Catholics are contained in the 31
Geo. III. c. 32, s. 7, and the 52 Geo. III. c. 155.

The period for the election of churchwardens is the
first week after Easter Sunday.   As a general rule, and
in the absence of a special custom applicable to a par-

* Non-residents having a "house of trade" in a parish are
liable to serve this office.

ticular parish, both the churchwardens are to be chosen by the incumbent and the parishioners; but if they differ about the persons to be appointed, then the incumbent is to choose one and the parish the other. In the greater portion of the London parishes, however, the parishioners by custom choose both; and a similar custom prevails in some country parishes, while in others the appointment is by a select vestry (see *post*) or by some class of the parishioners.

Churchwardens are elected by a show of hands on the part of those present in the vestry, unless a poll is demanded. It is then taken in accordance with the general rules which regulate voting in vestries, the former churchwardens in that case being the returning officers. If there be a disputed election, it is said that the bishop must swear in all the parties presented to him, leaving them afterwards to decide their rights by an action at law. And if the incumbent and parishioners omit to elect churchwardens, the Court of Queen's Bench will compel them by mandamus to do so. The same court will also grant a mandamus to compel the bishop to admit a churchwarden who has been duly elected.

Every churchwarden, before entering upon his office, must make and subscribe, in the presence of the bishop or archdeacon, a declaration faithfully and diligently to perform the duties of his office.

When sworn in, churchwardens remain in office, and are liable for the due performance of its duties, not only until their successors are appointed, but until the latter have made and subscribed the declaration required under 5 & 6 Wm. 4, c. 62,

s. 9.* Practically speaking, and indeed in accordance with one of the canons of the church, an election takes place annually in Easter week.

The personal property (goods, chattels, &c.) of the parishioners, so far as it is connected with the church, is vested in the churchwardens, who cannot, however, dispose of it without the consent of the parishioners. On the other hand, if they do dispose of them improperly, the parishioners cannot bring any action against them—that must be left to the churchwardens of the ensuing year.

The primary duty of the churchwardens is the care of the fabric of the parish church, of the fittings and ornaments thereof, and of the goods, chattels, utensils, &c., appertaining thereto. It is also their duty to preserve order and decorum in church during the performance of divine service. They may take off the hat of a person who refuses to do so when asked, and may turn out of church any one who misconducts himself or disturbs the service. By the canons they are required to see that all curates are duly licensed by the bishop, and that strangers, unless duly qualified, do not preach in the church. In case the incumbent is non-resident (without license), or is guilty of irregular or incontinent living, or of any misconduct calculated to bring the sacred office into contempt, it is their duty to present him at the annual visitation of the bishop. But if the minister introduces any irregularity into the service, *the churchwardens have no authority to interfere;* but they may and ought to repress all in-

* A declaration faithfully and diligently to discharge the duties of the office.

decent interruption of the service by others, and they desert their duty if they do not. At the same time, if ever the clergyman were guilty, either from natural infirmity or disorderly habits, of any act of a grossly offensive nature, either the churchwardens or any private persons might, in a case of absolute and immediate necessity, interpose to preserve the decorum of public worship.

The churchwardens have the care of the living during any period for which it may be vacant. On the death of an incumbent, or any other event which avoids it, it is their duty to apply to the chancellor of the diocese, who will authorize them to receive and manage the revenues of the living until a new incumbent is appointed. Out of the sums coming into their hands, they must pay a curate to perform the services of the church, and account for the balance to the new incumbent.

At the end of their year of office, or within a month afterwards, the churchwardens must, before the parson and parishioners in vestry assembled, present their accounts of receipts and disbursements. If they are allowed, an entry to that effect should be made in the church books, which must be signed by the parties allowing them ; and if any money remains in the hands of the outgoing churchwardens, it must be delivered over to their successors, together with the goods, &c., of the church, according to the inventory.* If any

* The ecclesiastical court can compel the production of their accounts ; but cannot dispute the validity of them when pre sented. The bishop, indeed, even although their accounts have been passed by the vestry, may cite them to give any further

churchwarden wilfully authorizes, or makes an illegal
or fraudulent payment from the church rate, or unlawfully makes any entry in his accounts for the
purpose of defraying or making up to himself, or any
other person, the whole or any part of any sum of
money unlawfully expended from the poor-rate, or. disallowed or surcharged in the accounts of any parish or
union by the district auditor, he may, upon conviction
therefor before two justices, be fined any sum not exceeding £20, and also treble the amount of such
payment or of the sum so entered in his accounts.
Churchwardens must allow an inspection of their
accounts by any parishioner who gives them a good
and substantial reason for desiring it. And, in case
of refusal, the Court of Queen's Bench will grant a
mandamus to compel their exhibition, on an applicant
stating a special reason why he wishes to examine
them. But there is no general right on the part of
individual parishioners to inspect the churchwardens'
books from motives of mere curiosity, or without
having some definite and legitimate object in view.

When passing their accounts, the payment of sums
of 40s. or above must be verified by vouchers, but
under that amount, the oath of the churchwardens is
held a sufficient verification.

As churchwardens cannot legally lay a rate to reimburse themselves for any expenses they have de-

statement he may desire with respect to the goods of the
church ; and if it appear that they have disposed of any portion of them without his assent, he may compel them to
replace them out of their own pockets, or otherwise punish
them.

frayed, they ought to be careful to provide for such expenses by a previous rate. If, indeed, they have actually laid a rate, but their receipts on account of it do not equal their disbursements before the expiration of their year of office, their successors may reimburse them out of such rate.

Agreements beneficial to the parish entered into by one set of churchwardens, with the consent of the vestry, will bind their successors and the parishioners.

These officers may bring actions for the recovery of goods belonging to the church, or for damage done to them. On the other hand, they may be sued in the Ecclesiastical Courts for neglect of duty; and, in case of misbehaviour, may be removed by those courts before the termination of their year of office. If, indeed, they take money, goods, &c., corruptly, under colour of their office, they may be indicted.

With respect to the duties of churchwardens in respect to the levying of church rates, see at a subsequent part of the work, the chapter on "CHURCH-RATES."

CHAPTER V.

OF THE CHURCH TRUSTEES.

UNDER the provisions of the act for the abolition of compulsory church-rates, passed in 1868, a new body, entitled church trustees, may come into existence in any parish, for the purpose of holding funds in trust for, and applying them to, certain purposes.

It is provided by that act, that a body of trustees

may be appointed in any parish for the purpose of accepting by bequest, donation, contract, or otherwise, and of holding any contributions which may be given to them for ecclesiastical purposes * in the parish.

The trustees are to consist of the incumbent and of two householders or owners or occupiers of land in the parish, to be chosen in the first instance, and also from time to time, on any vacancy in the office by death, incapacity, or resignation, one by the patron, and the other by the bishop of the diocese in which the parish is situate.

The trustees, when thus appointed, are a body corporate by the name of "the church trustees" of the parish to which they belong, having a perpetual succession and a common seal, with power to sue and be sued in their corporate name.

They may, from time to time, as occasion may require, pay over any funds in their hands to the churchwardens of the parish, to be applied by them—1. To the general ecclesiastical purposes of the parish. 2. To any specific ecclesiastical purposes of the parish.† The churchwardens must apply the funds to the purposes for which they are handed over to them; and due regard must be had in their application by the trustees

* In this act, "ecclesiastical purposes" means the building, re-building, enlargement, and repair of any church or chapel, and any purpose to which by common or ecclesiastical law a church-rate is applicable.

† It is expressly provided, that no power shall be hereby conferred upon the churchwardens to take order with regard to the ecclesiastical purposes of the parish further or otherwise than they were by law entitled to do before the passing of the act.

to the direction of donors who contributed them for any special ecclesiastical purposes. By "special ecclesiastical purposes" must, it would seem, be understood some one or more of the objects to which a church-rate may be applied.

The trustees are empowered to invest the funds in their hands in Government or real securities, and to accumulate the income thereof or otherwise deal with the funds as they think fit, subject of course to the provisions of the act.

The incumbent of the living is, *ex officio*, the chairman of the trustees, who are required once at least in every year to lay before the vestry an account of their receipts and expenditure during the preceding year, and of the mode in which such receipts have been derived and expenditure incurred; together with a statement of the amount, if any, of funds remaining in their hands at the date of such account.

CHAPTER VI.

THE PARISH CLERK, SEXTON, AND BEADLE.

ACCORDING to writers on ecclesiastical law, parish clerks were originally chosen from aspirants for the clerical office, whose poverty compelled them to accept this inferior office. Indeed, under an act of parliament passed in the present reign (7 & 8 Vict. c. 59, s. 2), a person in holy orders may now be employed to fill the office, receiving all the profits belonging thereto, and performing all its ecclesiastical duties. The election in that case is to be by the same persons as now have

the right to elect a parish clerk ; but no " clerk in
orders " (as he is called) is entitled to perform any of
the duties of the office nor to take any of its profits,
until licensed by the bishop. He is, moreover, removable in the same manner as a mere stipendiary
curate.

As a general rule, the clerk is appointed by the incumbent; but, in many parishes, there is a custom
that he should be elected by the parishioners or by the
incumbent, with the consent of the vestry, and such a
custom is perfectly good. The parish clerks of parishes
formed under the New Parishes Act, are always to be
appointed by the incumbent for the time being, while
they are removable (for misconduct) by him with the
consent of the bishop. The person appointed parish
clerk must be twenty years of age ; and, according to
a canon of the church, must possess competent skill
in reading, writing, and (if possible) in singing, although
this latter qualification does not appear to be indispensable. When elected or appointed, parish clerks
are usually licensed by the bishop, and take an oath to
obey the incumbent. This, however, is not necessary
to complete their title to their office. The emoluments
of the office vary according to the practice in each
parish ; as a general rule, they are chiefly derived from
fees payable upon the performance of the different
offices of the church.

The office of a parish clerk is a freehold ; * but by
the 7 & 8 Vict. c. 59, s. 5, if it appears, upon complaint or otherwise, to any archdeacon or other ordi-

* It does not, however, confer a county vote unless land to
the annual value of 40s. is attached to the office.

nary, that any person not in holy orders holding or
exercising the office of church clerk, chapel clerk, or
parish clerk, in any district parish or place subject to
his jurisdiction, has been guilty of any wilful neglect
or misbehaviour in his office, or that by reason of any
misconduct he is an unfit and improper person to hold
and exercise the same, such archdeacon, &c., may
summon such clerk to appear before him, and by
writing under his hand, or such process as is used in
the ecclesiastical courts for procuring the attendance
of witnesses, call before him all persons competent to
give evidence respecting the matters imputed to such
clerk; and may summarily hear and determine the
truth of the matters charged against him; and if on
such investigation it appears to the satisfaction of such
archdeacon, &c., that they are true, he may forthwith
suspend or remove such clerk from his office, and by
certificate under his hand and seal directed to the
officiating minister, declare the office vacant. A copy
of the certificate is to be affixed to the principal door
of the church, and the persons entitled to elect are
forthwith to elect another person in his place. But
the exercise of the office by a sufficient deputy who
duly and faithfully performs the duties, and in all
respects well and properly demeans himself, is not to
be deemed a wilful neglect of office on the part of the
clerk, so as to render him for that cause alone liable to
be suspended or removed.*

The right to appoint the sexton is very much regulated by the customs of different parishes, in some
being vested in the parishioners, in others in the

* Steer's Parish Law, by Hodgson, p. 145.

incumbent, and again, in a third case, in the church-wardens. It is laid down that, in the absence of proof of any custom, it will be presumed that the church-wardens have the right to appoint when it is the duty of this official to take care of the sacred vestments and of the church, but that when he has only to do with the churchyard, the presumption is in favour of the incumbent's right. In all cases, it would appear that the right of the inhabitants to elect must be made out by proof of a special custom in a particular parish. One curious point in connection with this office is, that not only may a woman be appointed sexton, but if the appointment is in the parishioners, women may vote at the election. The emoluments of the office depend, like those of the clerk, very much upon custom ; the principal source consists in fees.

As a general rule the duties of the sexton are thus defined in a work of authority :—he is " to keep the church clean swept and adorned, to open the pews, to make and fill up the graves for the dead, and to provide, under the direction of the churchwardens, candles and necessaries belonging to the church, to get the linen washed, &c., to keep out excommunicated persons, and generally to prevent any disturbance in the church."

At common law the sexton has a freehold in his office, and therefore, although the ecclesiastical courts may visit him with ecclesiastical censures if he mis-conducts himself, neither they nor any one else have power (unless there is a special custom to the contrary in the parish) to remove him. In parishes formed under the New Parishes Act, however, the sexton is to

be appointed by the incumbent, and to be removable
by him with the consent of the bishop.

The beadle of a parish is chosen by the vestry. It
is his duty to attend the vestry, and to inform the
parishioners when and where it is to be held, to act
as its messenger or servant, to assist the constable in
taking up beggars, passing vagrants, &c. Unless he is
regularly sworn in as a constable he cannot take or receive into his custody a person charged with any offence.
The beadle is only appointed during the pleasure of the
parishioners, and may at any time be dismissed by
the vestry for misconduct.

CHAPTER VII.

THE PARISH VESTRY.

THE parish vestry is the general assembly of the
parishioners, and it derives its name from the fact that
up to a very recent period it was always held in the
vestry or in the parish church. It is indeed, even now,
generally held in the vestry. But in consequence of
scenes frequently occurring at these meetings which
could hardly be considered befitting either the church
or even the vestry, power is given to the poor-law
commissioners (now the Local Government board), by
the 13 & 14 Vict. c. 57, to make an order that, at the
expiration of twelve months from the publication thereof, no vestry shall be held either in the church, or,
except in case of urgency, in the vestry. At the same
time, power is given to provide other places to hold the
meetings. But the poor-law board can only issue such

an order upon the application of the churchwardens, sanctioned by a resolution of the vestry.

The incumbent of the parish has a right, *ex officio,* not only to be present and to take part in every vestry meeting, but, further, to take the chair and preside over its deliberations. The persons entitled to attend and vote at a vestry are the ratepayers of the parish, whether resident or non-resident therein. No person, however, who has neglected or refused to pay any poor-rate which is due, and has been demanded from him, is enabled to attend or vote, or be present until he has paid the same.* It is not, indeed, necessary to have actually paid any poor-rate, for if a man have come into the parish since the last rate was laid, he can vote in respect of the property for which he has become liable to be rated exactly as if he had been actually rated. The non-payment of church-rates due and demanded does not, however, disqualify for attendance and voting at a vestry meeting held for the purpose of transacting, and while it is transacting, any business other than such as relates to the imposition or expenditure of a church-rate. But, by the Compulsory Church-rate Abolition Act, 1868, no person who makes default in paying the amount of a church-rate for which he is rated, shall be entitled to inquire into,

---

* This rule is subject, however, to a qualification introduced by the 16 & 17 Vict. c. 65, which enacted, that no person shall be required, in order to vote or be present at any vestry meeting under the provisions of the 58 Geo. 3, c. 69, and 59 Geo 3, c. 85, to have paid any rate for the relief of the poor of the parish in which such meeting shall be held, which shall have been made, or become due, within three calendar months immediately preceding such vestry meeting.

or object to, or vote in respect of the expenditure of
the moneys arising from such church-rate. And if
the occupier of any premises make default for one
month after demand in the payment of any church-
rate for which he is rated, the owner may pay the
same, and will, thereupon, be entitled, until the next
succeeding church-rate is made, to stand for all purposes relating to church-rates (including attending at
vestries and voting thereat) in the place in which such
occupier would have stood.

Vestry meetings, which may be held as often as the
parish business requires, are generally called by the
churchwardens with the consent of the incumbent.
By the 7 Wm. 4, & 1 Vict. c. 45, three clear days'
notice of the place and hour of holding the same, and
of the special purpose thereof, must be given by affixing a notice (signed by a churchwarden or by the
rector, vicar, or curate of the parish, or by an overseer) * to the principal doors of all the churches within
the parish previous to the commencement of divine
service on Sunday. And to remind the parishioners
that a meeting is to be held, it is usual to toll one
of the church-bells for half-an-hour before the time
of assembling.

As we have already said, the incumbent, if present,
is entitled to preside at a vestry meeting. If he is
not there, a chairman is to be chosen by those present,
voting in the manner we shall now describe.

Under the old common law, every ratepayer had a
single vote, and no more ; and this is, in fact, still the

---

* Vestries for church matters should regularly be called by
the churchwardens with the consent of the minister.

case when any question submitted to the vestry is decided, as it may be, by a show of hands.* But if the question before the meeting is one that may legally be entertained, a poll may always be demanded, at which all persons duly qualified may vote, whether they were present at the show of hands or not. The poll is now taken under the provisions of the 58 Geo. 3, c. 69, s. 3, which now regulates the voting in vestries, and whereby it is provided, "that every inhabitant present who, by the last rate made for the relief of the poor, shall have been assessed in respect of any annual rent, profit, or value not amounting to £50, shall give one vote and no more; if assessed for any such annual rent, &c., amounting to £50 or upwards (whether in one or more than one sum or charge), he is entitled to give one vote for every £25 in respect of which he shall have been assessed; but so that no inhabitant shall give more than six votes; and where two or more of the inhabitants present are jointly rated, each is to vote according to the proportion borne by him of the joint charge; and where only one of the persons jointly rated attends, he is to vote according to the whole of the joint charge." † Under the Poor rate Assessment and Collection Act, 1869, occupiers of small tenements let for short periods retain

---

* On a show of hands, a majority of those present must vote for any resolution in order to carry it. Persons refusing to vote cannot be treated as absent.

† Where a man is rated for property held by him in his individual capacity, and also for property held by him as executor, the two may be lumped together, so as to give him an additional vote for an additional £25 of annual value. *Reg.* v. *Kirby*, 31 L. J. Q. B., 3.

their votes in the vestry, although these rates may
be compounded for and paid by their landlords.
Where companies or corporations are rated to the poor,
their clerk, secretary, steward, or other agent, duly
authorized for the purpose, may (if their rates have
been duly paid) represent them at any vestry meeting,
and give the number of votes to which their property
entitles them.

If there is no other business before the vestry, the
poll should be taken immediately after it is demanded,
unless this should be attended with inconvenience; but
the chairman has a legal right to fix the time of the
poll. The poll must, if demanded on a show of hands,
be taken of the ratepayers generally. It is a nullity
if the poll is confined to persons present when it is
demanded. The doors of the vestry should be kept open
during the taking of the poll, for which sufficient time
must be allotted to allow all the ratepayers the opportunity of voting. And where there is a custom in any
parish, with reference to the period of polling, it must
be followed, provided it be reasonable.

When the votes are equal on a poll, the chairman
has a right to give a casting vote, in addition to the
vote or votes to which he is entitled as a private individual, in respect of his assessment.* The same section of the act (see below) which confers this power
upon the chairman, renders it imperative upon him to
sign the proceedings of the vestry, which are to be
entered in a book to be provided for the purpose by
the churchwardens and overseers.† Any inhabitants

* 58 Geo. 3, c. 69, s. 2.
† Section 6 of the act just quoted provides for the safe custody of the parochial books, and imposes penalties upon any

present who choose may likewise do so. Their signa-
tures are merely regarded as authenticating the record
of the proceedings, and do not involve them in any
personal responsibility, *unless the resolution or resolutions to which they set their names expressly guarantees*
the payment of expenses ordered to be incurred.

Speaking generally, the vestry "has the right to
investigate and restrain the expenditure of the parish
funds, to determine the expediency of enlarging or
altering the churches and chapels, or of adding to or
disposing of the goods and ornaments connected with
those sacred edifices. The election of some of the
parish officers is either wholly or in part to be made by
the vestry, and it has, either directly or indirectly, a
superintending authority in all the weightier matters of
the parish." *   It has, amongst other things, the power
to make or refuse a church rate. This general statement
of the powers of the vestry may here suffice, as we shall
have occasion to refer more particularly to the most important of its duties in subsequent portions of the work.†
It is only necessary further to remark, that every
parishioner, whether present or absent, is bound by a
vestry meeting duly called.   One vestry may, however,
rescind the proceedings of a previous one.

The vestry clerk is the secretary of the vestry by
whom he is elected. His duty is to attend its
meetings, to draw up its orders and resolutions, and

person obliterating or destroying them, or neglecting to produce them, when required, to the vestry or parochial officers.

* Steer's Parish Law, by Hodgson, p. 289.

† With respect to the election of churchwardens by the
vestry, see *ante*, Chapter IV.

generally (although the vestry may order otherwise) to keep the parish books. The duties of this officer are, indeed, much more minutely defined when he is (as is no doubt generally the case) appointed under the 13 & 14 Vict. c. 57. That act gave the Poor-law commissioners (now the Local Government board) power to order the appointment of a vestry clerk in all parishes whose population exceeded 2,000 at the last census, the appointment to be made within one month after the issuing of such order, or (on subsequent occasions) after the vacancy of the office, and seven clear days' notice being given of the vestry meeting convened for the purpose. Sect. 7 defines the duties of such vestry clerk (unless otherwise ordered by the commissioners), and as this officer is one of great importance in all populous parishes, we shall give the clause nearly entire. He is, then, "to give notice of, and attend, meetings of the vestry and committees appointed thereat. To summon and attend meetings of the churchwardens and overseers when required, and to enter the minutes thereof. To keep the account of charity moneys distributed by the churchwardens or overseers. To keep the vestry books, parish deeds, &c., rate books· and accounts which are closed, and to give copies of, and extracts from, the same at the rate of fourpence for seventy-two words, and to permit all ratepayers of the parish to inspect them at reasonable times, on pain of dismissal for neglect. To make out, when required by the vestry, the church rate, and procure it to be signed and completed, and to retain the custody thereof, and where there is no collector of poor rates or

E

assistant overseer, to make out the poor rate and procure its allowance, and to make all subsequent entries
in the rate books, and to give the notices thereof
required by law. To prepare and issue the necessary
process for recovering arrears of such rates, and to
procure the summons to be served, and to attend the
justices thereon, and to advise the churchwardens and
overseers as to the recovery of such arrears. To keep
and make out the churchwardens' accounts, and to
present them to the vestry or other legal authority to
be passed, and to examine the church rate collector's
accounts, and returns of arrears. To assist the overseers in making out their accounts (whenever required
by them), and, subject to the rules of the Poor-law
commissioners, to examine the accounts of the assistant overseers and collectors of poor rates and their
returns of arrears. To attend the audit of overseers'
accounts, and conduct all correspondence arising therefrom. To assist the churchwardens and overseers in
preparing and making out all other parochial assessments and accounts, and in examining the accounts
of the collectors of such assessments. To ascertain
and make out the list of persons liable to serve on
juries, and to cause them to be duly printed and
published and returned to the justices. To give
the notices for claims to vote for members of parliament, to make out lists of voters and get them
printed and published and duly returned according to
law, to attend the revising court, and to prepare, make
out, and publish the business lists and lists of constables. To make all returns required of the churchwardens or overseers by law or proper authority. To

advise the churchwardens and overseers in all the duties of their office, and to perform such other duties and services of a like nature as the Poor-law commissioners from time to time, at the request of the churchwardens or overseers, or otherwise, may prescribe and direct." By sect. 9 it is declared, however, that nothing in that act is to exempt or discharge any churchwarden or overseer from the performance of any duty required of him by law, or to oblige him to avail himself of the assistance of the vestry clerk unless he thinks fit to do so.

Vestry clerks not appointed under the 13 & 14 Vict. c. 57, are removable at any vestry meeting, and no salary is attached to their office.

Vestry clerks appointed under the act to which we have just referred, are not removable from office, except by a resolution passed at a vestry called for that special purpose, and with the consent of the Local Government board ; or by an order under the seal of such board. The salary of such clerks is fixed by the order directing their appointment, and is charged upon the poor rate. On the other hand, they must give such security as the Local Government board order.

CHAPTER VIII.

SELECT VESTRIES.

A "SELECT vestry" consists of a certain number of persons chosen annually to manage the concerns of the parish. In some parishes, the establishment of such a body is the result of immemorial usage, which in that case fixes also its constitution and mode of election; the latter in some cases being that worst of all kinds of election—self-election. When it is sought to support by custom the existence of a select vestry in a parish, and thus to exclude the parishioners from the direct—or it may even be the indirect—management of their own affairs, the said custom must be shown—

1 To have existed immemorially.*
2. To have existed continuously; *i. e.* as to the *right*. For a mere interruption in the *exercise* of the right will not destroy the custom.
3. To have been acquiesced in peaceably by the parishioners.
4, 5, and 6. To be reasonable, compulsory, and consistent.

The existence of a custom for a select vestry must, if contested, be tried before one of the common-law courts.

In addition to the select vestries by custom, such bodies often exist in virtue of private and local acts relating to particular parishes. Those acts, of course, regulate their constitution and mode of election.

There are also the select vestries under the 59 Geo. 3, c. 12 s. 1 (commonly called Sturges Bourne's Act). These do not, however, replace the open vestry in the general government of the parish. Their duties are entirely confined to the administration of the poor laws,

---

* A custom is said to have existed "immemorially" when it cannot be shown to have commenced since the beginning of the reign of Richard I.: and in the absence of such proof a jury are entitled to infer the existence of an "immemorial custom" from the usage of the previous twenty years.

with which the "parish vestry," whether open or select, has no concern.

The 1 & 2 William 4, c. 60 (commonly called Hobhouse's Act) enables parishes, being part of a city or town, and containing a population of more than 800 persons rated as householders, to adopt that act if they think fit, and elect under its provisions a select vestry for the general management of all such their local affairs as would otherwise be within the jurisdiction of the open vestry. If it is desired to adopt the act, one-fifth of the ratepayers, who must be at least fifty in number, must deliver a requisition (in a form given in the act) to the churchwardens between the 1st of December and the 1st of March, requiring them to ascertain whether a majority of the parishioners wish the act to be adopted. Then, on the first Sunday in March, the churchwardens are to fix a notice on the doors of all the churches and chapels within the parish, specifying the day (not earlier than ten nor later than twenty-one days after such Sunday), and the place where the ratepayers are to vote for or against the adoption of the act. The voting is to take place by a written or printed declaration addressed to the church-wardens. If two thirds of the votes given (the whole number of persons voting being a clear majority of the ratepayers of the parish) are in favour of the adoption of the act, the said act (due notice having been given of its adoption) becomes the law for the election of vestrymen and auditors, which is henceforth to take place annually in May—the voters being such persons as have been rated to the poor for one whole year preceding their voting, and have paid all rates,

&c., except those becoming due within six months of each voting. The vestry is to consist of resident householders rated to the poor on a rental of not less than £10 per annum, and to be 12 in number where the number of rated householders does not exceed 1000; 24 where it exceeds 1000; 36 where it exceeds 2000; and so on, in the proportion of 12 for every 1000; but in no case is the whole number of vestry-men to exceed 120, unless, indeed, a greater number is fixed by any special act of parliament. The rector, district rectors, vicar and perpetual curate, are to be part of, and vote in, such vestry in addition to the elected vestrymen. One-third of the members of the vestry (who are, however, eligible for re-election) are to go out of office each year. The vestry elected under this act is to exercise the powers and privileges held by any vestry existing in the parish at the time of the passing of that measure. And various clauses contain provisions as to the vestry-room, the chairman, the accounts, auditors, &c., for which we must refer our readers to the act itself.

CHAPTER IX.

METROPOLITAN VESTRIES.

THE election and powers of the vestries in the metropolis are now regulated by the 18 & 19 Vict. c. 120, commonly called the "Metropolis Local Management Act," and by the 25 & 26 Vict. c. 102, "the metropolis" being defined therein to consist of the city of

London, and parishes and places comprehending an area from Hampstead on the north to Woolwich and Lewisham on the south, and from Stratford-le-Bow on the east to Hammersmith on the west.*

The vestry in every parish included in this area is to consist of—18 vestrymen, where the number of rated householders does not exceed 1000; † 6 additional (*i. e.* 24 vestrymen) where the number exceeds 1000; and 12 additional (*i. e.* 36 vestrymen) where the number of rated householders exceeds 2000; and so on, in the proportion of 12 additional vestrymen for every 1000 rated householders. In no case are the elected vestrymen to exceed 120.‡ To them are to be added the incumbent and churchwardens of the parish, and any district rector who is a member of the vestry of such parish at the time of the passing of the act. Parishes which, at the time of the act passing, contained upwards of 2000 inhabitants, are to be divided into wards, none of which must contain fewer than 500 rated householders; the secretary of state for the home

* The act also empowers the Queen in council, upon the application of the metropolitan board of works, to order the provisions of the act to be extended to any parish adjoining the metropolis containing not fewer than 750 inhabitants rated to the relief of the poor.

† If there are not eighteen persons in a parish qualified to be vestrymen, the vestry is to consist of as many as are qualified.

‡ The qualification requisite for a vestryman is, under ordinary circumstances, an assessment to the relief of the poor upon a rental of not less than £40; but in case the number of such assessments is not equal to one-sixth of the whole assessments in any parish, the qualification of a vestryman for that parish is reduced to £25.

department apportioning the vestrymen amongst the wards. One-third of the vestry go out of office every year,* so that every vestryman serves three years, except such as are elected to supply vacancies occasioned otherwise than by effluxion of time. In that case they are to go out of office at the times when the terms of office of the members in whose place they are elected would have expired by effluxion of time.

The election of one-third of the vestry, in place of that which retires, takes place annually in May, the electors being such persons as have been rated in such parish to the relief of the poor for one year next before the election, and have paid all parochial rates, taxes, and assessments, except church rates, due from them at the time of so voting, except such as have been made or become due within six months immediately preceding. Of course, when vacancies in the vestry occur by death or resignation, there will be bye-elections to supply them, which may take place at any part of the year.

On the day of election, the parishioners rated for the relief of the poor † in the parish or ward for which the election is holden are to meet at the place appointed for the election, and to nominate two ratepayers of the parish or ward to be inspectors of votes,

---

* Retiring vestrymen are eligible for re-election.

† Occupiers of tenements may claim to be rated by serving notice upon the overseers or one of them ; and this whether their landlord has or has not been, is or is not liable to be, rated for such tenements ; or has or has not compounded for the rates due on the same. If the rates have been compounded for, the tenant is only liable to pay the amount of composition due for the tenement he occupies.

and the churchwardens, or, in case of a ward election, such one of the churchwardens as is present thereat, or, if one of the churchwardens is not present, the person appointed to preside, is to nominate two other such ratepayers to be inspectors. The parishioners present are then to proceed to the election of vestrymen and also of auditors, unless five or more ratepayers require a poll, which, if demanded, is to take place on the following day, commencing at 8 A.M., and terminating at 8 P.M. At this poll, which must be taken by ballot, *each ratepayer has one vote and no more.* By the 25 & 26 Vict. c. 102, s. 36, the inspectors of votes may, before commencing the duties of their office, appoint by writing under their hands an umpire ; and in case the inspectors are unable to agree upon or determine by a majority any matter which they are by the said act required to determine, such matter is to be decided by the umpire, whose decision in relation thereto is to be final and conclusive.

If on the poll two or more persons appear to have an equal number of votes, the inspectors are to decide by lot which of them are to be returned as elected. When the election is complete, the list of persons elected vestrymen and auditors must be returned by the inspectors of votes to the churchwardens, who will publish it to the parish in the manner appointed by the act.

Section 11 of the act provides for the auditing of the parish accounts.

The persons thus elected as *vestrymen,* together with the persons added in virtue of their offices,* form the

* See *ante,* p. 55.

vestry, and (*with two exceptions,* which we shall presently mention) "all the duties, powers, and privileges,
including such as relate to the affairs of the church, or
the management or relief of the poor, or the administration of any money, or other property applicable to
the relief of the poor, which might have been performed or exercised by any open, or elected, or other
vestry, or any such meeting as aforesaid (*i. e.* a meeting
of parishioners), in any parish, under any local act, or
otherwise, at the time of the passing of the 18 & 19
Vict. c. 120, are to be deemed to have become transferred
to and vested in the vestry constituted by that act,"
i. e. "the Metropolis Local Management Act."

The *two exceptions* to which we have just referred
are—1st, as to the election of churchwardens and the
imposition of church rates. For it is enacted by an
act (the 19 & 20 Vict. c. 112, s. 1) passed in the
year after the Metropolis Local Management Act,
that when the power of electing churchwardens or
making church rates, or rates in the nature of church
rates, was, at the passing of the 18 & 19 Vict. c. 120,
vested in an open vestry, or in any meeting in the
nature of an open vestry meeting, or in any meeting
of the parishioners, inhabitants, or ratepayers, such
power is not to be deemed to have vested in the vestry
elected under the Metropolis Local Management Act.
2nd. Various powers, heretofore exercised by the vestry,
are, by the Metropolis Local Management Act, transferred, in certain parishes, to the district boards of works
to be appointed under that act.

Sect. 28 of the 18 & 19 Vict. c. 120, provides that, in order to constitute a quorum at any

meeting of a vestry elected under this act, there must be not fewer than five vestrymen present at a meeting of a vestry which consists of not more than 18 elected vestrymen; and not less than 7 present at a vestry consisting of 24 elected vestrymen and no more; and not less than 9 present at a vestry consisting of 36 elected vestrymen or upwards. Sect. 9 provides for the giving due notice of meetings of the vestry. While sect. 30 enacts that at every meeting of the vestry, in the absence of the persons authorized by law or custom (*i. e.* generally the incumbent or one of the churchwardens), the members present shall elect a chairman for the occasion before proceeding to other business; and that the chairman, in case of an equality of votes on any question, is to have a second or casting vote.

Various parishes of the metropolis, enumerated in a schedule to the act, are then grouped into districts, over each of which a board of works (the number of whose members is fixed by the act) is to preside. The board is to be composed of deputies elected by the vestries of the various parishes in the district. One-third of their number go out of office every year, the vacancies being supplied by the election of the vestries.

The vestries of parishes which are not included in districts* and the district boards are constituted corporations, and are enabled to hold land for the purposes of the act.

Superior to both vestries and district boards is "the Metropolitan Board of Works," which, like the two

* These—the vestries of the largest parishes—are virtually district boards, having all the powers of the latter bodies.

inferior bodies, is a corporation with power to hold lands. It is composed in the following manner:—the corporation of the city of London elect three members; the vestries of certain parishes named in a schedule to the act, each elect either one or two members; the boards of works of districts set forth in another schedule, each return one member; while other boards of works are united for the election of a joint representative. One-third of the members of the board retire from office each year, and the place of any member dying, resigning, or otherwise ceasing to be a member, is supplied by the board or vestry by whom he was originally elected. The metropolitan board is empowered to appoint a chairman, with a salary of not less than £1500, nor more than £2000 a year.

One very important clause in the act disqualifies certain persons from being members of any of the metropolitan boards or vestries. It enacts in substance, that any member of the metropolitan or any district board, or any auditor, who becomes bankrupt or insolvent, or compounds with his creditors, or accepts or holds any office under the board or vestry of which he is a member, or of whose accounts he is auditor (except in the case of an auditor, of the office of auditor), or is in any manner concerned or interested in any contract or work made with or executed for such board or vestry, is to cease to be a member or auditor. But no shareholder in a joint-stock company is to be disabled from continuing or acting as a member of a board or vestry by reason of any contract between such company and such board or vestry, or of any work executed by such company; but no such member is to vote upon any question in which such company is interested. Any person acting as a member of a board or vestry, or as auditor, after ceasing to be such member or auditor, or being a shareholder in a company who votes upon any question in which the company is interested, and any person acting as a member of a vestry without being duly qualified, is liable to a penalty of £50. But all acts and proceedings of any person ceasing to be a member or auditor, or disabled from acting, if done previously to the recovery of the penalty, are valid.

The members of all the metropolitan representative bodies are enabled to resign their offices at any time; and all of them are capable of immediate re-election after going out of office.

The act contains a number of provisions regulating with considerable minuteness their proceedings, the appointment of committees and officers, the provision of offices, &c.; but for these, we must refer our readers to the act itself, as any attempt to summarize them would occupy more space than we can spare for a subject which is of a local although it may be a metropolitan character. For the same reason we must confine ourselves to stating generally that the act gives powers to the bodies we have named to make and maintain sewers;* to pave, cleanse, and light the streets; and to remove and prevent nuisances. In general, it may be said that they have powers similar

* To the metropolitan board is committed the duty, as most of our readers are no doubt aware, of carrying out a plan of drainage for the whole metropolis.

to those which in most large towns are either possessed by the corporations under the Municipal Corporation Act, or have been conferred upon them by
successive improvement acts.

In conclusion, we have to refer to the mode in which
the funds for carrying out the act are to be provided.
Every vestry and district board may, by order under
their seal, require the overseers of their parish, or of
the several parishes within their district, to pay to the
treasurer, or into any bank, the sums required for defraying the expenses of the execution of the act, dis-
tinguishing the sums connected with sewerage, and
also with lighting (when land is exempted, or is rated
at a less rate than houses for lighting under any act
of parliament), from the other expenses.   The overseers
to whom such order is issued, are to levy the amount
required by making separate sewer rates, lighting rates
(when a sum is required for that purpose), and a general rate.   These rates are to be levied on the person,
and, in respect of the property rateable to the relief of
the poor, assessed on the net annual value of such property, and allowed in the same manner and subject to
the same appeal as poor rates.*

The metropolitan board obtains the sums it may
require by precepts addressed to the vestries and
district boards.

Borrowing powers are conferred by the act upon all
the bodies to which we have been referring.

* See *post*, the chapter on poor rates.

CHAPTER X.

OF CONSTABLES.

High constables were formerly appointed for each hundred, wapentake, or other like division of a county. The office is now, however, practically extinct, except in cases where the high constable is, by law or custom, returning officer at any parliamentary or municipal election, or is charged with the supervision of the register of electors, or has any real property vested in him by virtue of his office. These exceptional instances need not detain us. We pass on to what are more properly within the scope of the present work— parish constables.

These are now appointed in accordance with the provisions of the 5 & 6 Vict. c. 109, according to the sixth section of which all able-bodied men, *resident* * within the parish, between the ages of twenty-five and fifty years, rated to the relief of the poor or to the county rate for any tenement of the net yearly value of four pounds or upwards (except such persons as are exempt or disqualified, as will be mentioned immediately afterwards), are qualified and are liable to be appointed parish constables.

The following persons are exempt from liability

* A mere occupier of a tenement, for which he pays rent, rates, and taxes, was never liable, because this is an office requiring personal attendance, and the holder of it should be well known to the inhabitants.

to be appointed parish constables :—All peers; all
members of the House of Commons; all judges of the
superior courts; all justices of the peace; all deputy
lieutenants; all clergymen in holy orders; all Roman
Catholic priests; all dissenting ministers who shall follow no secular occupation except that of a schoolmaster,
producing a certificate of some justice of the peace
of their having taken the oaths and subscribed the
declarations required by law ; all schoolmasters; all
serjeants and barristers-at-law actually practising ; all
members of the society of doctors of law and advo-
cates of the civil law actually practising; all attorneys,
solicitors, and proctors duly admitted in any court of
law or equity or of ecclesiastical or admiralty jurisdiction, in which attorneys, solicitors, and proctors have
been usually admitted, actually practising and having
duly taken out their annual certificates ; all convey-
ancers and special pleaders below the bar ; all officers
of any such courts actually exercising the duties of
their respective offices ; all coroners, gaolers, and keepers
of houses of correction ; all members and licentiates of
the Royal College of Physicians in London actually
practising ; all surgeons being members of one of the
Royal Colleges of Surgeons in London, Edinburgh, or
Dublin, and actually practising ; all apothecaries having
obtained a certificate to practise as an apothecary from
the master, wardens, and society of the city of London,
and actually practising; all officers of Her Majesty's
navy or army on full pay; all persons enrolled and
serving in any corps of yeomanry under officers having
commissions from Her Majesty, or lieutenants of counties or others specially authorized by Her Majesty for

that purpose; all pilots licensed by the Trinity house of Deptford, Stroud, Kingston-upon-Hull, or Newcastle-upon-Tyne; and all masters of vessels in the buoy and light service employed by either of those corporations; all pilots licensed by the lord warden of the cinque ports, or under any act of parliament or charter for the regulation of pilots in any other port; all the household servants of Her Majesty; all officers of customs and excise; all sheriffs and sheriffs' officers; all high constables; the clerks of all boards of guardians of the poor; the masters of all union workhouses; all county or district constables; all parish clerks; all registrars and superintendent registrars of births, deaths, and marriages; all churchwardens, overseers, and relieving officers; and all postmasters and persons employed in the business of the post-office.

The above persons are *exempt* from liability to serve this office, *i. e.* they need not serve unless they choose; but all licensed victuallers and persons licensed to deal in any exciseable liquor or to sell beer by retail, all gamekeepers, and all persons who have been convicted of any treason, felony, or any infamous crime are *disqualified* from serving the office, *i.e.* they cannot serve it.

Within the first seven days of February in each year the justices of the division in which each parish is situated issue a precept to the overseers in that parish directing them to make out a list of all persons therein qualified to serve as parish constables, and return the same to the justices before the 24th of March. The overseers, within fourteen days after they have received the precept, call a vestry meeting, who make out a list of the persons in the parish qualified

F

and liable to serve (with the Christian name and sur-
name and true place of abode, the title, quality, calling
or business of each written at full length), and they
may annex to this the names of any number of
persons willing to serve the office of constable, and
whom they recommend to be appointed, although they
may not have the requisite qualifications. The overseers present this list (verifying it on oath, and attending to answer any question touching the same) to
a special sessions of the justices of the peace of the
division holden for the purpose on some day between
the 24th of March and the 9th of April in each year.
And from the list as amended by striking out the
names of all disqualified, not liable, and not consent-
ing to serve, or disabled by lunacy or imbecility of
mind, or by deafness, blindness, or other infirmity of
body, the justices select the names of such number of
persons as they deem necessary (having regard to the
extent and population of the parish) to act as constables within the parish, and until other constables
are chosen and sworn to act in their stead, as constables
for such parish ; provided always, that where any person
has been chosen to serve, and has served the office of
constable, either in person or by substitute, he is not
liable to be again chosen until every other person in the
parish liable and qualified to serve has also served the
office of constable either in person or by substitute. The
persons thus nominated serve for a year, or until their
successors are appointed, unless previously removed
from office by the justices for misconduct or some other
good cause. Before entering upon their duties they
must, however, attend on a day to be named in order

to be sworn. And all persons who, being duly appointed, and being qualified and liable to serve, refuse
to do so, and fail to provide a qualified substitute (who
need not be on the list approved by the vestry), is, upon
conviction before two justices, to be fined not more than
£10; and every person who, after being sworn as constable, refuses, or wilfully neglects, to act in the execution of his office, is, upon conviction before two justices, to forfeit for such offence not more than £5.

The act, after directing that the lists of the parish
constables should, within fourteen days after their
appointment, be affixed by the overseers to the doors
of the parish church; and providing (by section 16)
for the filling up of any vacancies which may occur in
the course of a year by the death, disqualification, or
discharge of any constable during his year of office;
authorizes the justices, on the resolution of the parish
vestry, to appoint, in aid of the regular parish constables *who are unpaid,** a certain number of paid constables for each parishes.

The parish constables are subject to the authority of
the chief constable of the county constabulary for the
county, or the superintendent of the district in which
they are situated. These officers cannot, however, call
upon them to serve beyond the boundaries of their own
parishes.

In addition to the ordinary constables appointed as
we have described, *special constables* may also be appointed under the 1 & 2 Wm. 4, c. 41. By the first
section of that act, when it is made to appear to two

* Except by fees for the performance of certain duties, such
as the service of summonses, execution of warrants, &c.

justices of any county or town, on oath, that any
tumult, riot, or felony has taken place, or may be
apprehended, in any parish, &c., for which they act,
and they think the ordinary peace officers insufficient
for the protection of persons and property, they may
appoint, by precept under their hands, as many householders or other persons (not legally exempt from
serving the office of constable) residing in such place,
or in the neighbourhood, as they think fit, to act as
special constables.   Such special constables are to take
an oath.   The secretary of state may order persons
who are exempt from service as constables to be sworn
in.   While acting, such constables have all the powers
of common constables.   And any special constable
convicted before two justices of refusing to take the
oath, or of neglecting to appear at the proper time and
place for taking it, or of neglecting to serve when
called upon, or to obey lawful orders, is liable to a
penalty of £5.   The justices in whom the appointment of special constables is vested may determine
their service; when they must deliver up the staves
and other articles provided for them, on penalty of a
sum not exceeding £5.   The justices, at a special sessions to be held for the purpose, may order reasonable
allowances and expenses to be paid to, or on account
of, the special constables.   And by the Municipal Corporations Act (5 & 6 Wm. 4, c. 76, s. 83) the justices
in a municipal borough are empowered to call out special constables within its limits.

Such are the main provisions of the acts which
regulate the appointment of parish and special constables.   They are not repealed by the other acts,

which provide what may be considered, under ordinary circumstances, the active police of the country, the borough police, and the county constabulary.* The former (the borough police) are established under the Municipal Corporations Act (5 & 6 Wm. 4, c. 76), which authorizes every town council to appoint, out of their own body, a certain number of persons, who, with the mayor for the time being, are to be " the watch committee," and are to appoint constables to be sworn in before a justice having jurisdiction in the borough. These constables (*i. e.* the borough police) are to have, within the borough, and also within the county in which the borough they are appointed for is situated, all the powers and privileges, and are to be liable to all the duties and responsibilities, which any constable has within his constablewick (*i. e.* the district for which he is appointed constable) by virtue of the common law or any statute.

The county constabulary are established under three acts of parliament (2 & 3 Vict. c. 93, 3 & 4 Vict.

* When, under the 5 & 6 Vict. c. 109, a precept had been issued by justices ordering overseers to make out and return a list of men qualified and liable to serve as parish constables, and the overseers had duly called a meeting of the inhabitants for the purpose of making out such list, but the inhabitants assembled at the meeting declined to do so in consequence of thinking it unnecessary that any such constables should be appointed, a mandamus was granted ordering them to make out and return the list. The justices are the persons to determine whether parish constables shall still be appointed in places where the rural police system is established ; and if in the exercise of their discretion they think fit to issue their precept, the inhabitants must obey it.—*The Queen* v. *the Inhabitants of North Brierley*, 27 L. J. M. C. 275.

c. 88, and 19 & 20 Vict. c. 69), which, taken together,
require the justices of every county, or (with the
approbation of the secretary of state) for a division of
a county, to establish a county police, to be under the
command of a chief constable for the county or division of a county, and, subordinate to him, under-
superintendents, who are to have districts allotted to
them. The chief constable, subject to the approval of
two or more justices in petty sessions, is to appoint the
other constables, and a superintendent for each police
division of the county, and may dismiss them at pleasure.
Subject to the directions of the justices in quarter sessions, he has also the general command of the police
force. The expenses of the force are to be paid out
of a police rate, to be made by the justices in quarter
sessions, and to be levied with the county rate; the
Treasury contributing one-fourth of the expense on the
certificate of one of their inspectors that the force is in
an efficient condition. Besides the regular police force,
who are always out, are paid regular wages, and are
at the orders of the chief constable for such service,
falling within the duties of police, as he may direct,
the chief constable is to make out a list of fit persons
in every parish, &c., within each petty sessional division, who are willing, in case of need, to serve as *local
constables*. The list is to be laid before the justices at
one of the special sessions for hearing appeals against
the poor rate, who are to select from the list so many
local constables as they think fit, and to cause an oath
to be administered to them. Tables of fees and allowances for the service of summonses and warrants, and
the performance of other duties by the local constables,

are to be settled by the secretary of state. We shall not refer further to the provisions of the acts under which the county constabulary is established, as they scarcely belong to our subject. It was, however, necessary to give this brief outline of them, in order to exhibit the relation in which the *parish constables* stand to the general police of the kingdom. And we shall quit this part of the subject with the remark, that all constables—parish constables, special constables, local constables, and police constables—are under the direction and subject to the orders of the chief constable of the county, division, or borough, in which is situated the district for which they are appointed.

It only remains for us to state—and it must necessarily be very briefly and generally—the powers, duties, and privileges of all classes of constables.

A constable cannot take into custody, without a warrant from the justices, persons who are insulting each other, or have struck each other, unless they actually strike or offer to strike each other in his presence. Then he may take them into custody.

If persons are committing an affray in a house, or if there be a noise, or disorderly drinking therein at an unreasonable time of the night, or if persons having committed felony, or made an affray, fly to the house and are immediately pursued, a constable, after declaring the cause of his coming, and having previously demanded admission in vain, may break open the doors to arrest the offender or suppress the affray.* A constable (indeed this is also true of any private person)

* 2 Hale, P. C. 117. Steer's Parish Law, by Hodgson, p. 393.

may, or rather is bound to, apprehend any offender in
the act of committing a felony.   Any person whatever,
and of course constables, are authorized by the 14th &
15th Vict. c. 19, s. 11, to apprehend persons found
committing any indictable offence in the night, *i. e*
from 9 P.M. to 6 A.M.

A constable, *having reasonable cause to suspect* that
a person has committed a felony, may, and indeed
should, apprehend, and detain him until he can be
brought before a justice to have his conduct investi-
gated.

Constables refusing. or neglecting, on due notice
or on their own view, to assist in carrying before
a justice of the peace hawkers and pedlars trading
without a licence, or refusing to produce their licence,
or in executing the warrants of justices against such
offenders, are to forfeit £10.   Constables also incur
penalties for neglecting to apprehend vagrants.   And
they are further required to assist a landlord in
the day-time in breaking open any house, barn, &c.,
where the goods of a tenant are clandestinely removed, or fraudulently concealed for the purpose of
levying a distress ; but in case the place where they
are suspected to be concealed is a dwelling-house, oath
must first have been made before a justice of a reasonable ground of suspicion.

A constable is *bound* to execute the warrant of a
justice of the peace within his own *precinct* (*i. e.* the
district for which he is appointed, which in the case of a
parish constable is the parish), whether the warrant be
directed to him by name or generally to the constable or
peace officer of that precinct.   And in order to execute

a warrant, a constable is in general justified in breaking open outer doors or other parts of a house *after* but *not before* he has declared his business, demanded admission, and allowed a reasonable time for opening them to elapse. But he is, on the contrary, *not* justified in breaking open outer doors to execute a warrant of distress for a poor rate, or for a church rate. And the constable should take care to have the warrant with him when he executes it, since he is bound to show it on the demand of the party on whom it is to be executed. The officer should afterwards keep the warrant for his own justification.

It is, in general, the duty of a constable, when once he has apprehended a person, to retain him in custody for the purpose of taking him with all convenient speed before a justice of the peace. If, however, he has taken him into custody for a mere trivial affray, he may liberate him when the heat is over. And, until he can take a prisoner before a justice, he may confine him in a house or the gaol of the place.

A constable enjoys certain privileges. While serving the office, he is not liable to be appointed to any other. His person, while engaged in the discharge of his duty, is specially protected; and persons assaulting him, with intent to resist the lawful apprehension or detainer of offenders, may be sentenced to imprisonment, with or without hard labour, for any time not exceeding two years, and may also be fined and required to find sureties to keep the peace. He possesses, also, some advantages in the defence of actions brought against him for acts done in the performance of his duty. And no actions of this kind can be brought against him, unless they are commenced within six months after the act committed.   On the other hand, if he neglect his duty to suppress an affray or riot, or to apprehend a felon, &c., he is guilty of a misdemeanor, for which he may be indicted and punished with fine and imprisonment.

By the 18 Geo. 3, c. 19, every constable, within fourteen days after he goes out of office, is to present to the overseers of the parish an account of all sums received and expended by him on account of the parish.   The overseers are, within fourteen days afterwards, to lay this before the inhabitants, and, if approved by the majority of them, any amount due to him is to be paid out of the poor rate.   If the account is disallowed, the constable has an appeal to a justice of the peace; and so on the other hand have the parish.   Both parties can appeal from the justice to the next quarter sessions. The constable can only, it must be remembered, charge for actual expenses incurred in doing the business of the parish.

It will be understood that we have in this chapter confined ourselves, as far as possible, to the law affecting the *parish constable*.   We have here nothing to do with the organization of the borough and county police, which are not parochial forces.   Information with respect to them must be sought in the acts under which they are established.   So far as relates to the general duties of constables in apprehending offenders, executing warrants, &c., to the penalties imposed upon neglect, or their protection against assault or actions for acts done in discharge of their duty, the same law is applicable to all peace officers.

CHAPTER XI.

OF THE PREPARATION OF JURY LISTS.

IN the first week of July in each year, the clerk of the peace in each county issues his warrant, requiring the churchwardens and overseers to prepare, before the 1st September, lists of all persons in their respective parishes liable to serve on juries.

The churchwardens and overseers having made out such a list, are, on the three first Sundays in September, to fix a copy thereof upon the principal door of every public place of religious worship in their parishes or townships, with a notice stating when and where the objections to the list will be heard by the justices. The list must specify which of the persons whose names are contained in it are, in the judgment of the overseers, qualified as special jurors, and must also set forth in each case the nature of the qualification, and also the occupation and the amount of the rating or assessment of every such person. The latter hold a special sessions for the revision of these lists in the last seven days of September.

The churchwardens and overseers, and also the justices in petty sessions, are authorized to inspect the tax assessment for any parish or township between the 1st July and 1st October in every year, for the purpose of making out or revising the jury list. And any constable, churchwarden, or overseer offending against the act by neglect of duty or otherwise, may be fined

not more than £10, nor less than 40s. by the justices
before whom he may be summoned.

CHAPTER XII.

OF HIGHWAYS.

HIGHWAYS or public roads are those ways which all
the Queen's subjects have a right to use. It is said
that there are three kinds of public ways :—a footway,
a foot and horseway, and a foot, horse, and cartway.
Whatever distinctions, however, may exist between
these ways, it seems to be clear that any of them
which are common to all the Queen's subjects, whether
directly leading to a market town, or beyond a town,
or from town to town, or village to village, may properly be called a highway. A common street is also
a highway, so is a navigable river, and so also a towing-
path by its side, although only used for that purpose.
A turnpike road is also a highway, although open to
the public only on payment of tolls; and although its
maintenance is provided for otherwise than is the case
with respect to highways in general. It was at one time
a question whether there could be a public highway
which is not also a thoroughfare. It is, however, now
settled, that there is no reason in point of law why
a place which is not a thoroughfare should not be a
highway, if there has been such a use of it by the
public as will lead to the inference that it has been
dedicated to the public use for that purpose. At the
same time, it must be admitted that the fact of its not

being a thoroughfare would be a strong argument
against any road being a highway.

Roads are highways, either in virtue of prescription,
i. e. of their having been open to the public since the
period of legal memory ; or from their dedication to
the public use by the owner of the soil. This may
take place either by express declaration, or by some
act showing on his part an intention to give the public
irrevocable licence to travel along it at their free will
and pleasure. His permitting it to remain freely open
to the public traffic for some time, is one of the
strongest indications to this effect. Thus, where the
owners of the soil suffered the public to have the free
passage of a street in London, though not a thoroughfare, for eight years without any impediment (such as
a bar set across the street and shut at pleasure, which
would show the limited right of the public), it was
held a sufficient time for presuming a dedication of the
way to the public. So where a street communicating
with a public road at each end had been used as a
public road for four or five years, it was held the jury
might presume a dedication. In a case where it ap-
peared that a passage leading from one part to another
of a public street (though by a very circuitous route),
made originally for private convenience, had been open
to the public for a great number of years without any
bar or chain across it, and without any interruption
having been given to persons passing through it, it
was ruled that this must be considered as a way
dedicated to the public. But the erection of a bar to
prevent the passing of carriages, rebuts the presumption
of a dedication to the public, although the bar may

have been long broken down; and though such a bar
do not impede the passing of persons on foot, no public
right to a footway is acquired.

In every case, the facts must be such as are sufficient
to show that the owner meant to give the public a
right of way over his soil, before a dedication by him
will be presumed. And nothing done by a lessee or
tenant without the consent of the owner of the land,
will give a right of way to the public.

It seems that there may be a partial dedication of a
way, although doubts have been entertained on the
subject. Where, for instance, the owner of an estate
permitted the public to use a road for several years for
all purposes except that of carrying coals, Mr. Justice
Bayley and Mr. Justice Holroyd thought that there
was ground for presuming such a dedication as would
constitute a high road for all purposes except the carrying of coals.

The greater number and the most important of the
highways throughout the kingdom are what are called
turnpike-roads, on account of their having been either
originally formed under, or subsequently regulated by,
acts of parliament which have provided the means of
keeping them in repair by tolls taken at the turnpikes
erected upon them. Parishes are not, however, exone-
rated from the liability to repair such roads when they
have existed immemorially; though it is not often requisite to resort to them for such a purpose, as the
funds vested in the trustees are generally sufficient to
meet all necessary expenses of this description. But,
by 4 & 5 Vict. c. 59, s. 1 (continued by 17 & 18
Vict. c. 52), a power is given to justices at a special

sessions for the highways, when the funds of a turnpike trust are insufficient for the repairs of the road,
to examine the state of the resources and debts of the
trust, and to inquire into the state and condition of the
repairs, and if they think fit to do so, to order what
portion (if any) of the rate to be levied, under the
5 & 6 William 4, c. 50 (the Highway Act), shall be
paid to the trustees or their treasurer, by the surveyor
of the parish, township, or other district maintaining
its own highways.

The inhabitants of the parish at large are by common
law bound to repair all highways lying within it, unless
by prescription or otherwise they can throw the burthen
upon particular persons. No mere *agreement*, however, can exonerate a parish from this common law
liability.

But although nothing more than a dedication by the
owner of the soil is requisite to give the public a right
to the use of a highway, nor is anything more requisite
to cast upon the parish the duty of repairing all ways
which have so become highways *before* the passing of
the Highway Act (4 & 5 William 4, c. 50), yet, as
to highways created *after* the passing of that act, the
liability of the parish to repair is materially limited;
for, by the 23rd sect., it is enacted that " no road or
occupation way made or hereafter to be made by and
at the expense of any individual or private person,
body politic or corporate, nor any roads already set
out or to be hereafter set out as a private driftway
or horsepath, in any award of commissioners under
an inclosure act, shall be deemed or taken to be a
highway, which the inhabitants of any parish shall be

compellable or liable to repair, unless the person, body politic or corporate, proposing to dedicate such highway to the use of the public, shall give three calendar months' notice in writing to the surveyor, of his intention to dedicate such highway to the use of the public, describing its situation and extent, and shall have made or shall make the same in a substantial manner, and of the width required by this act, at the expense of the party requiring such view, which certificate shall be enrolled at the quarter sessions holden next after the granting thereof; then and in such case, after the said highway shall have been used by the public, and duly repaired and kept in repair by the said person, body politic or corporate (*i. e.* the person, body politic or corporate, dedicating it to the public), for the space of twelve calendar months, such highway shall for ever thereafter be kept in repair by the parish in which it is situate; provided, nevertheless, that on receipt of such notice as aforesaid, the surveyor of the said parish shall call a vestry meeting of the inhabitants of such parish, and if such vestry shall deem such highway not to be of sufficient utility to the inhabitants of the said parish to justify its being kept in repair at the expense of the said parish, any one justice of the peace, on the application of the said surveyor, shall summon the party proposing to make the new highway, to appear before the justices at the next special sessions for the highways to be held in and for the division in which the said intended highway shall be situate; and the question as to the utility, as aforesaid, of such highway, shall be determined at the discretion of such justices."

Two things must be borne carefully in mind with respect to this enactment:—1st. It only applies to roads which had not become highways chargeable on the parish before the passing of the act (31st August, 1835); and 2nd. A new road dedicated to the public after the passing of the act, may become a highway for all purposes, except that of chargeability upon the highway rate, although it has not been adopted on behalf of the public in the manner prescribed in the above section.

Although the whole parish is *primâ facie* bound to repair all the highways within its boundaries, yet a particular district of a parish *may* be liable by prescription to repair its own roads; or an individual may be liable to repair a highway by reason of his tenure of certain lands; or the owner of land by the side of the highway, not anciently enclosed, may, if he encloses it, become liable to repair the highway; for he thus takes away the liberty and convenience which the public have, of going upon the adjoining land when the highway is out of repair.* And, under the 62nd sect. of the Highway Act, arrangements may be made by the justices at the special sessions (the assent of the vestry having been previously obtained), for the transfer, upon such terms as may be agreed upon, of the liability of repairing particular highways from individuals or corporations, to the parish.

If a highway is in two or more parishes, each is individually liable for the repair and indictable for the non-repair of that portion within its boundaries. And to

* He may, however, relieve himself of the liability by throwing his land open again.

prevent the inconvenience which frequently arose where
the boundaries of parishes passed across or through the
middle of a common highway, and one side of such
highway was situated in one parish and the other side
in another parish, the fifty-eighth section of the Highway Act gives the justices, at a special sessions for the
highways, power " to divide the whole of such highway
by a transverse line crossing it, into equal parts or into
such unequal parts and proportions as in consideration
of the soil, waters, floods and inequality of the highway,
or any other circumstances attending the same, they in
their discretion think just and right, and to declare,
adjudge, and order that the whole of such highway on
both sides thereof, in any of such parts, shall be repaired by one of such parishes, and that the whole
thereof on both sides in the other of such parts shall
be maintained and repaired by the other of such
parishes."

We have now to consider who are the officers
charged with the care of the highways, what are the
powers with which they are invested, and what are the
means placed at their disposal   These points are now
regulated by the General Highway Act (5 & 6 Wm. 4,
c. 50), to which we have already so often referred ; by
the Public Health Act (11 & 12 Vict. c. 63, s. 117) ;
by the Local Government Act, 1858 (21 & 22 Vict.
c. 98, s. 12) ; and by the new Highway Act, 1862
(25 & 26 Vict. c. 61), amended by the 27 & 28
Vict. c. 101.   It will be convenient to take these acts
in their order, and show the various hands in which,
under one or other of them, the care and control of
the highways may be lodged.

1. *Under the General Highway Act,* 1835.—By the sixth section it is enacted that the inhabitants of every parish maintaining its own highways, at the first meeting in vestry for the nomination of overseers of the poor in every year, shall proceed to the election of one or more persons to serve the office of *surveyor or surveyors of highways* in the said parish for the year ensuing. In parishes where there is no meeting for the nomination of overseers of the poor, the inhabitants contributing to the highway rate are to meet at their usual place of public meeting upon the 25th day of March, or if that should happen to be a Sunday or Good Friday, then on the day next following, or within fourteen days after the said 25th day of March in every year, to elect one or more persons to serve the office of surveyor to the said parish. A poll must be taken if demanded. The qualification for the office of surveyor of highways is the ownership (either in his own right or that of his wife) of houses or land of the annual value of £10, or of personal property to the value of £100; or the occupation (whether resident in the parish or in any adjoining one) of houses, lands, &c, of the yearly value of £20. Persons exempted from serving as overseers are not compellable to act as surveyors, but others being duly qualified must either serve or provide a sufficient deputy, show good cause why they should not be appointed, or pay a fine not exceeding £20, to be imposed by any two justices.

The majority of the inhabitants of the parish in vestry assembled, may, if they think fit, appoint a single person of skill and experience to act as surveyor of highways *at a salary.*

If the vestry neglect to appoint a surveyor or surveyors, the justices at a special sessions for the highways may do so, or if the person appointed by the vestry dies, becomes disqualified, or neglects his duties during his year of office, the justices may appoint another person, either with or without salary, to fill the office until the next annual election of surveyor. When a parish is situated in more than one county, division, or liberty, the surveyor is to be appointed by the justices at a special sessions for the highways assembled in that county, division, or liberty, in which the church of the parish is situated.

This act also contains provisions enabling parishes to be united and districts to be formed for the management of their highways, but as these enactments have hitherto been, and are likely to remain, practically a dead letter, it is unnecessary to do more than refer to them here. They are contained in clauses 13 to 17, both inclusive.

The Highway Act also contains a very important provision, enabling large parishes to appoint a board for the management of their highways. By section 18, and subsequent sections, it is enacted that, in any parish where the population by the last census exceeds 5000, if it is determined by a majority of two-thirds of the votes of those present at the annual vestry meeting to form a board for the superintendence of the highways of the said parish, and for the purpose of carrying the provisions of the Highway Act into effect, the vestry may nominate and elect any number of persons not exceeding twenty nor less than five, being respectively householders, and residing in, and assessed to the rate for the relief of the poor of, the said parish, and also liable to be rated to the repair of the highways in the said parish, under and by virtue of this act, to serve the office of surveyors of the highways for the year ensuing; and such persons so nominated and elected, or any three of them, are to act as a board, and be called "the board for the repair of the highways of the parish of ———" (as the case may be), and to carry into effect the powers, authorities, and directions in this act contained.

2. *Under the Public Health Act.*—The local board of health, within the limits of their district, shall, exclusively of any other person whatsoever, execute the office of and be surveyor of the highways, and have all such powers, authorities and liabilities, as any surveyor of highways was at the time of the passing of the Public Health Act, or might thereafter be invested with, or be liable to by virtue of his office, by the laws in force for the time being, except in so far as such powers, duties, or authorities are or may be inconsistent with the provisions of the Public Health Act, 1848 (11 & 12 Vict. c. 63, s. 117). For the mode in which districts are formed under this measure, we must refer our readers to the act itself.

3. *Under the Local Government Act,* 1858 (21 & 22 Vict. c. 98, s. 24).—The duty of carrying into execution the Local Government Act, 1858, is vested in a local board consisting of (1) in corporate boroughs, the mayor, aldermen and burgesses, acting by the council; (2) in other places under the jurisdiction of a board of improvement commissioners, the board of commissioners; (3) in other places, such number of

elective members as may be determined by a resolution
of the overseers and ratepayers at a meeting held for
the purpose of adopting the act.   Local government
boards subject to the act under which they are constituted have all the powers, rights, duties and liabilities of local boards of health; including, of course,
the jurisdiction over the highways.

4. *Under the Highway Act,* 1862 (25 & 26 Vict.
c. 64).—By this act (amended by another passed in
1864) provision is made for the constitution of highway districts and highway boards.   Of these we shall
treat separately, as their importance seems to demand,
in the next chapter.   We shall note in the proper
place some points in which the Highway Act of 1835
is not applicable to these boards and districts.   But,
subject to the provisions of the Highway Act, 1862,
the statement of general highway law in the present
chapter will not be affected by the nature of the local
body in whom the management of the roads is vested.
As a rule, whatever be the body, its duties, powers,
and liabilities are the same.   It is necessary to bear in
mind, that when during the remainder of this chapter,
we speak of "the Highway Act" simply, we refer to
the act of 1835.

The duties of the surveyor or board of highways in
any parish are—to repair and keep in repair the parish
highways; to erect direction posts or boundary stones;
to remove impediments arising from falls of snow, or
from slips of the banks by the sides of the highway;
to levy highway rates; and duly to keep accounts of
receipt and expenditure, and present them to the vestry
within fourteen days after the appointment of the sur-

veyor or board for the ensuing year. These accounts
must subsequently be laid before the justices at a highway sessions to be holden within a month after the
annual election of surveyors.* And if any person chargeable to the highway rate has any complaint against such
accounts, or the application of the moneys received by
the surveyor, he may then complain to the justices,
who must hear the complaint, examine the surveyor
upon oath, if they think fit, and make such order as
the case requires. It is also the duty of the surveyor
of the highways, at the special sessions for the highways held next after the 25th day of March in each
year, to verify his account, and to make a return in
writing of the state of all the roads, common highways, bridges, causeways, hedges, ditches, and watercourses, appertaining thereto; and of all nuisances
and encroachments (if any) made upon the several
highways within the parish for which he was surveyor,
as well as the extent of the different highways which
the parish is liable to repair, what part thereof has
been repaired, with what materials, and at what expense; and what was the amount levied during the
time he was surveyor of the said parish.

If a person who has filled the office of surveyor of
highways dies before he has paid over to his successor
the money remaining due from him to the parish; or
before handing over the books, papers, tools, instru-
ments, and materials connected with his office; then,
in case of non-payment of such money, or non-deli-
very of such books, &c., for one calendar month after

* These provisions, with reference to accounts, are not applicable to the boards instituted under the Highway Act, 1862.

demand made by the succeeding surveyor, the latter may bring an action against the executors of his predecessor for such unpaid moneys, or for damages for the detention of the books, papers, tools, &c.

If any surveyor, district surveyor, or assistant surveyor, neglects his duty in anything required of him by the Highway Act for which no particular penalty is imposed, he is to forfeit for every such offence a sum not exceeding £5. And if the surveyor has any part, share, or interest, directly or indirectly, in any contract or bargain for work or materials, to be made, done, or provided, for or on account of any highway, &c., under his care; or uses or lets any team; or uses, sells, or disposes of, any materials to be used in making or repairing such highway, &c. (except by the licence of two justices in special sessions), he is to forfeit a sum not exceeding £10, and to be for ever incapable of being employed as a surveyor, with a salary, under the act.

We have spoken frequently of "the special sessions for highways." These are, of course, held by the justices of the petty sessional division of the county in which a parish is situate; and, by the Highway Act, the justices of each division, or any two or more of them, are required to hold not less than eight nor more than twelve special sessions in every year, for executing the purposes of this act; the days of the holding thereof to be appointed at a special sessions to be holden within fourteen days after the 20th March in each year.

The means of defraying the expenses connected with the repair and management of the highways of a parish are to be provided by a rate, which the surveyor is authorized to assess upon all property liable to be rated and assessed to the relief of the poor, together with all woods, mines, and quarries of stone, or other hereditaments, as have heretofore been rated to the highways. The rate cannot, however, be enforced until it has been allowed and signed by two justices of the peace. Highway rates, indeed, made by a local board of health acting as the surveyors of a district, under the 11 & 12 Vict. c. 63, need not be allowed or signed by the justices. In parishes where the overseers have power to compound for the payment of poor rates with the owners, instead of the occupiers, of certain classes of property, and in case of their refusal to compound, to rate such landlords as the occupiers, the surveyor of the highways has similar powers as to the highway rate. And by the 13 & 14 Vict. c. 99, s. 1, the vestry of any parish may order that the owners of tenements, the yearly value of which does not exceed £6, shall be rated to the highway rate instead of the occupiers; such assessment being at three-fourths the amount at which such tenements would otherwise have been rated. The justices may excuse payment of highway rates on account of poverty. But generally the surveyor has the same power, remedies, and privileges for levying and recovering the highway rate as the overseers of the poor have for the recovery of the poor rate. With the assent of the vestry, he may appoint rate-collectors, who are to be paid such allowances out of the highway rates as he may think reasonable; are to give security for the due and honest performance of their duties; and account to the surveyor when and as the latter directs.

We have now to consider the modes in which the repair of highways may be enforced. These are—1st.

By order of a special highway sessions; and 2nd. By indictment at the quarter sessions or assizes for the county. And—

1. *By order of special sessions.*—By the 94th section of the Highway Act it is provided, that if any highway is out of repair, and information thereof, on the oath of one credible witness, is given to any justice of the peace, he is required to issue a summons requiring the surveyor of the parish, or other person, body politic or corporate, chargeable with such repair, to appear before the justices, at some special sessions for the highways, in the summons mentioned, to be held within the division in which the said highway is situate; and the said justices are either to appoint some competent person to view the same, and report thereon to the justices in special sessions on a certain day and place to be then and there fixed, at which the said surveyor of the highways, or other party as aforesaid is to be directed to attend, or the justices are to fix a day whereon they or any two of them shall attend to view the said highway, and if it appears to the justices at such special sessions, on the day and at the place so fixed, either on the report of the person appointed to view, or on the view of such justices, that the highway is not in a state of thorough and effectual repair, they are at such special sessions to convict the surveyor, or other party liable, in a penalty not exceeding £5; and to order the surveyor or other person, &c., to repair such highway in a limited time; and in default of such repairs being effectually made within the time limited, the surveyor or other person, &c., is to forfeit and pay to some person to be named and

appointed in a second order, a sum of money to be
therein stated, and equal to the sum which the said
justices judge requisite for repairing such highway;
such money to be recoverable in the same manner as
any forfeiture,* and to be applied to the repair of the
highway. In case more persons than one are bound
to repair the highway, the justices are to direct what
proportion shall be paid by each of the said parties.
If the highway out of repair is part of a turnpike
road, then the justices are to summon the treasurer or
surveyor, or other officer of such turnpike road, and
then an order is to be made on such treasurer or surveyor, or other officer as aforesaid, and the money
therein stated is to be recoverable as aforesaid.

This method of proceeding is only available when
the duty or obligation of the surveyor, &c., to repair
the highway in question (supposing it to be out of repair) is not disputed. If that once comes in question,
it must be decided under the next mode of proceeding :—

2. *By indictment.*—The 95th section of the act to
which we have just referred, provides that if, on the
hearing of such a summons as that which we have just
described, respecting the repair of any highway, the
duty or obligation of making such repairs is denied
by the surveyor on behalf of the inhabitants of the
parish, or by any other party charged therewith, the
justices are to direct an indictment to be preferred, and

* By distress warrant against the goods and chattels of the
surveyor ; or if he has no goods and chattels, then he may be
committed to prison for a period not exceeding three calendar
months (with hard labour), unless the fine is sooner paid.

the necessary witnesses in support thereof to be sub-
pœnaed, at the next assizes for the county, or at the
next general quarter sessions for the county, riding,
division, or place, wherever such highway shall be,
against the inhabitants of the parish or the party named
in such order, for permitting the highway to be out of
repair.*

The right to present an indictment, either against
the parish or the surveyor, for the non-repair of a
highway, is not limited to the case contemplated in
the above section.   Any individual may present such
an indictment, whether he has or has not taken proceedings before the justices, and whether the duty of
the parish to repair the highway in question be or be
not questioned.

If it appear on the trial, either that the highway in
question is not out of repair, or that the parties indicted are not liable to repair it, they will be acquitted;
if both these facts are found against them, they will be
convicted.   The judgment in the latter case usually is,
that they pay a fine and repair the road.   But upon a
certificate of a justice of the peace, that the road is
in good condition at the time judgment is about to be
pronounced, the court will merely assess a nominal
fine.   In all cases, the fine is to be applied to the repair of the highway.

The nuisances to highways form a subject which our
space will compel us to discuss very briefly.   There is
no doubt that all injuries whatever to a highway, as

* An information *may* also be filed against a parish in the
Court of Queen's Bench ; but practically this remedy is little
resorted to.

by digging a ditch, or making a hedge across it, or laying logs or timber in it, or by doing any other act which will render it less commodious to the Queen's subjects, are public nuisances at common law; and as such the party causing them is indictable at the quarter sessions or assizes. Thus, if the tenant of land plough the land over which others have a way, this is a nuisance, for the way is rendered not so easy as before. If a man with a cart use a common " pack and prime way," so as to plough it up and render it less convenient, that is also a nuisance, and indictable. If there be a stile across a public foot-way, and a man raises this stile to a greater height, this is a nuisance. And it is clearly a nuisance to erect a new gate across a highway, though it be not locked, and open and shut freely. It is also a nuisance to suffer the highway to be incommoded by reason of the foulness of the adjoining ditches, or by boughs of trees hanging over it.

For these, and such like obstructions, not only may an indictment be presented on behalf of the public, but further, if any individual suffers from one of them any peculiar injury besides that which is inflicted upon him as one of the public, he may bring an action for it.

An indictment, however, is a very cumbrous remedy for all offences of this description which do not cause permanent injury to a highway, or involve some disputed question of right which it is desirable to have settled by the most competent court. The Highway Act, therefore, enables the surveyor to summon before the justices of the peace—who are authorized to inflict pecuniary fines upon them—persons causing or committing the most usual obstructions or offences to or

upon highways. Thus sects. 64 to 67 provide for the
removal or pruning of trees which injure the highway.
Sect. 69 imposes a fine for encroachments. Sect. 70
forbids under a penalty the making of pits or shafts,
or the erection of steam-engines, wind-mills, lime or
brick-kilns, &c., within a . certain distance of a highway. Sect. 73 relates to the removal of matters laid on
the highway; while sect. 72 condenses in itself so much
of what may be called the every-day police of a highway, that it will be convenient to give it entire. It enacts
that " if any person wilfully rides upon a footpath or
causeway by the side of any road made or set apart for
the use or accommodation of foot passengers; or wilfully leads or drives any horse, ass, sheep, mule, swine,
or cattle, or carriage of any description, or any truck
or sledge upon any such footpath or causeway; or
tethers any horse, ass, mule, swine, or cattle, upon any
highway, so as to suffer or permit the tethered animal
to be thereon; or cause any injury or damage to be
done to the highway, or to the hedges, posts, rails,
walls, or fences thereof, or wilfully destroys or injures
the surface of any highway; or wilfully or wantonly
pulls up, cuts down, removes or damages the posts,
blocks, or stones fixed by the surveyor as herein directed; or digs or cuts down the banks which are the
securities and defence of the highways, or breaks,
damages, or throws down the stones, bricks, or wood
fixed upon the parapets or battlements of bridges, or
otherwise injures or defaces the same; or pulls down,
destroys, obliterates or defaces any milestone, or post
graduated, or direction post or stone erected upon any
highway; or plays at foot-ball, or any other game upon

any part of the said highways, to the annoyance of any passenger or passengers ; or if any hawker, juggler, gipsy, or other person travelling, pitches any tent, booth, stall, or stand, or encamps upon any part of any highway; or if any person makes or assists in making any fire, or wantonly fires off any gun or pistol, or sets fire-to or wantonly lets off or throws any squib, rocket, serpent, or other firework whatsoever, within fifty feet of the centre of such carriage-way or cart-way ; or baits, or runs for the purpose of baiting, any bull upon or near any highway ; or lays any timber, stone, hay, straw, dung, manure, lime, soil, ashes, rubbish, or other matter or thing whatsoever, upon such highway, to the injury of such highway, or to the injury, interruption, or personal danger of any person travelling thereon ; or suffers any filth, dirt, lime, or other offensive matter or thing whatsoever, to run or flow into or upon any highway from any house, building, erection, lands, or premises adjacent thereto ; or in any way wilfully obstructs the free passage of any such highway ;—every person so offending shall for each and every such offence forfeit and pay any sum not exceeding 40s. over and above the damages occasioned thereby."

Under sect. 51 of the Highway Act the surveyor of the highways is entitled to dig materials for the repair thereof in any waste land or common ground, river or brook within the parish. Sect. 54 entitles him (if sufficient cannot be had conveniently in such waste land, &c.), with the licence of a special sessions, to get materials in enclosed lands or grounds not being a garden, yard, avenue to a house, lawn, park, paddock, or enclosed plantation not exceeding 100 acres in extent. (One calendar month's notice of his intention to do so must be given, sect. 53.)

The widening, stopping, and diverting of highways, are the last points which will engage our attention. By sect. 80 of 4 & 5 Will. 4, c. 50, the surveyor of highways is required to make, support, and maintain, or cause to be made, supported, and maintained, every public cart-way, leading to any market town, twenty feet wide at least, and every public horse-way eight feet wide at the least, and to support and maintain every public foot-way by the side of any carriage-way or cart-way, three feet at the least, if the ground between the fences will admit thereof. But the surveyor is not required to make a public foot-way without the consent of the vestry.

By sect. 82 two justices of the peace may upon view order a highway to be widened, so that it do not exceed thirty feet in breadth, and that in its enlargement no house or building be pulled down, or any part of a garden, park, paddock, lawn, yard, nursery, &c., be taken. Compensation to be made out of the highway rate for the land thus taken, and if the surveyor and the owner cannot agree as to the value, this is to be assessed by a jury.

Sects. 84 and 85 enable two justices to order (subject to subsequent confirmations by the quarter sessions) a highway to be stopped up, diverted, or turned either entirely, or reserving a bridle-way or footway along the whole or any part thereof, on the application of the surveyor of the highways, with the consent of the inhabitants of the parish in vestry assembled. They also prescribe minutely the course of procedure to be adopted with this view. And by sect. 88 any person believing that he would be aggrieved by any such order to divert or stop up a highway, may appeal against it to the quarter sessions. If the jury then find that "the proposed new highway is nearer or more commodious to the public, or that the public highway so intended to be stopped up, either entirely or subject as aforesaid, is unnecessary, or that the party appealing would not be injured or aggrieved," the appeal will be dismissed, and the order of the justices below confirmed. But if a different verdict is returned on any of these points, the order will be quashed. If no appeal is entered, the order of the justices will, of course, be confirmed.

CHAPTER XIII.

OF HIGHWAY DISTRICTS UNDER THE HIGHWAY ACTS OF 1862 AND 1864.

UNDER two recent Acts of Parliament,* passed in 1862 and 1864, provision is made for the division of England into highway districts. The formation of such districts is not, however, compulsory, but is left to the discretion of the justices.

It is of course impossible for us, in the space at our disposal, to give a complete analysis of these important acts; but it is believed that nearly all the leading points will be found included in the following summary.

* 25 & 26 Vict. c. 61, and 27 & 28 Vict. c. 101.

Any five or more justices of a county may, by writing, under their hands, require the clerk of the peace to add to or send with the notice required by law to be given of the holding of courts of general or quarter sessions a notice that, at the court therein mentioned, a proposal will be made to the justices to divide the county or some part thereof into highway districts, or to constitute the whole or some part thereof a highway district. The justices assembled at the court of general or quarter sessions mentioned in the notice may then entertain such proposal, and make a provisional order dividing their county or some part thereof into highway districts, or constituting the whole or some part of their county a highway district, for the more convenient management of highways, but this order will not be valid unless it is confirmed by a final order of the justices assembled at some subsequent court of general or quarter sessions. And when it is proposed that only a part of a county shall be divided into a highway district, not less than two out of the five justices making such proposal must be resident in the said district, or acting in the petty sessional division in which such district, or some part thereof, is situate.

The justices making a provisional order under this act are to appoint some subsequent court of general or quarter sessions, to be held within a period of not more than six months, for taking into consideration the confirmation of the provisional, by a final, order.

The justices assembled at the appointed court of general or quarter sessions may make a further order —quashing the provisional order, or confirming it with or without variations, or respiting the consideration of such provisional order to some subsequent court of general or quarter sessions.

The provisional order is to state the parishes to be united in each district, the name by which the district is to be known, and the number of waywardens (such number to be at least one) which each parish is to elect.

There must not be included in any highway district formed in pursuance of these Acts any of the following places : that is to say, any part of a county to which the act passed in the session holden in the 23rd and 24th years of the reign of Her present Majesty, chap. 68, and intituled *An Act for the better Management and Control of the Highways in South Wales,* extends : The Isle of Wight : Any district constituted under the Public Health Act, 1848, and the Local Government Act, 1858, or either of such Acts : Any parish or place the highways of which are at the time of the passing of this act, or may be within six months afterwards under the superintendence of a board established in pursuance of section 18 of the Highway Act, 1835, unless with the consent of such board: Any parish or place within the limits of the metropolis as defined by the act passed in the session holden in the 18th & 19th years of Her Majesty, chapter 120, and intituled *An Act for the better Local Management of the Metropolis :* Any parish or place, or part of a parish or place, the highways whereof are maintained under the provisions of any local act of parliament. And no parish or place, or part of a parish or place, within the limits of a borough, can be included in any highway district formed in pursuance of this act without the consent, firstly, of the council of such borough, and secondly, of the vestry of the parish which, or part of which, is proposed to be included.

The highway board of each highway district consists of the waywardens elected in the several places within the district, in the manner we shall presently describe, and of the justices acting for the county and residing within the district.

The following are the regulations with respect to the election of waywardens in highway districts:—

In every parish forming part of a highway district there shall be elected every year for the year next ensuing a waywarden or such number of waywardens, as may be determined by order of the justices.

Such waywarden or waywardens shall be elected in every parish forming part of a highway district at the meeting and time, and in the manner, and subject to the same qualification and the same power of appointment in the justices in the event of no election taking place, or in the event of a vacancy, at, in, and subject to which a person or persons to serve the office of surveyor would have been chosen or appointed if this Act had not passed.

The justices shall in their provisional order make provision for the election of a waywarden or waywardens in places where no surveyor or surveyors were elected previously to the place forming part of a highway district.

A waywarden shall continue to act until his successor is appointed, and shall be re-eligible.

The highway board of a district are at their first

meeting or at some adjournment thereof by writing
under their seal, to appoint a treasurer, clerk, and district surveyor; they may also at any meeting, if they
think fit, appoint an assistant surveyor.

The following are the most important provisions of
the Highway Act, 1862,* with respect to the "works
and duties" of the boards :—

The highway board shall maintain in good repair
the highways within their district, and shall, subject
to the provisions of this act, as respects the highways
in each parish within their district, perform the same
duties, have the same powers, and be liable to the same
legal proceedings as the surveyor of such parish would
have performed, had, and been liable to if this act had
not passed. It shall be the duty of the district surveyor to submit to the board at their first meeting in
every year an estimate of the expenses likely to be
incurred during the ensuing year for maintaining and
keeping in repair the highways in each parish within
the district of the board, and to deliver a copy of such
estimate, as approved or modified by the board, so far
as the same relates to each parish, to the waywarden of
such parish.

Where complaint is made to any justice of the peace
that any highway within the jurisdiction of the highway board is out of repair, the justice shall issue two
summonses, the one addressed to the highway board,
and the other to the waywarden of the parish liable to
the repair of such highway, requiring such board and
waywarden to appear before the justices at some petty
sessions, in the summons mentioned, to be held in the

* 25 & 26 Vict. c. 61, secs. 17-19.

division where such highway is situate; and at such
petty sessions, unless the board undertake to repair the
road to the satisfaction of the justices, or unless the
waywarden deny the liability of the parish to repair,
the justices shall direct the board to appear at some
subsequent petty sessions to be then named, and shall
either appoint some competent person to view the highway, and report to them on its state at such other
petty sessions, or fix a day, previous to such petty
sessions, at which two or more of such justices will
themselves attend to view the highway.

At such last-mentioned petty sessions, if the justices
are satisfied either by the report of the person so
appointed, or by such view as aforesaid, that the highway complained of is not in a state of complete repair,
it shall be their duty to make an order on the board
limiting a time for the repair of the highway complained of; and if such highway is not put in complete
and effectual repair by the time limited in the order,
the justices in petty sessions shall appoint some person
to put the highway into repair, and shall by order
direct that the expenses of making such repairs,
together with a reasonable remuneration to the person
appointed for superintending such repairs, and amounting to a sum specified in the order, together with the
costs of the proceedings, shall be paid by the board;
and any order made for the payment of such costs
and expenses may be removed into the Court of
Queen's Bench, in the same manner as if it were an
order of general or quarter sessions, and be enforced
accordingly.

All expenses so directed to be paid by the board

in respect of the repairs of any highway shall be
deemed to be expenses incurred by the board in
repairing such highway, and shall be recovered accordingly.

The highway board may appear before the justices
at petty sessions by their district surveyor or clerk, or
any member of the board.

When, on the hearing of any such summons respecting the repair of any highway, the liability to
repair is denied by the waywarden on behalf of his
parish, or by any party charged therewith, the justices
shall direct a bill of indictment to be preferred, and
the necessary witnesses in support thereof to be sub-
pœnaed, at the next assizes to be holden in and for
the said county, or at the next general quarter sessions
of the peace for the county, riding, division, or place
wherein such highway is situate, against the inhabitants of the parish, or the party charged therewith,
for suffering and permitting the said highway to be
out of repair; and the costs of such prosecution shall
be paid by such party to the proceedings as the court
before whom the case is tried shall direct; and if
directed to be paid by the parish shall be deemed to
be expenses incurred by such parish in keeping its
highways in repair, and shall be paid accordingly.

The salaries of the officers appointed for each district, and any other expenses incurred by any highway
board for the common use or benefit of the several
parishes within such district, shall be annually charged
to a district fund to be contributed by and charged
upon the several highway parishes within such district
in proportion to the rateable value of the property in

each parish, but the expenses of maintaining and keeping in repair the highways of each highway parish within the district, and all other expenses legally payable by the highway board in relation to such parish, including any sums of money that would have been payable out of the highway rates of such parish if the same had not become part of a highway district, except such expenses as are in this act authorized to be charged to the district fund, shall be a separate charge on each parish.*

If any person feels aggrieved by any rate levied on him for the purpose of raising moneys payable under a precept of a highway board on the ground of incorrectness in the valuation of any property included in such rate, or of any person being put on or left out of such rate, or of the inequality or unfairness of the sum charged on any person or persons therein, he may appeal to the justices in special sessions.

Where any waywarden of a highway parish of a district, or any ratepayer of such parish feels aggrieved in respect of the matters following :—

1. In respect of any order of the highway board for the repair of any highway in his parish on the ground that such highway is not legally repairable by the parish, or in respect of any other order of the board, on the ground that the matter to which such order relates is one in regard to which the board have no jurisdiction to make an order ;

2. In respect of any item of expense charged to the separate account of his parish on the ground that such

* 27 & 28 Vict. c. 101. See the immediately following sections of the same act as to the mode of levying rates, &c.

item of expense has not in fact been incurred or has been incurred in respect of a matter upon which the board have no authority by law to make any expenditure whatever;

3. In respect of any item of expenditure charged to the district fund on the ground that such item of expense has not in fact been incurred, or has been incurred in respect of a matter upon which the board has no authority by law to make any expenditure whatever;

4. In respect of the contribution required to be made by each parish to the district fund on the ground that such amount, when compared with the contribution of other parishes in the district, is not according to the proportion required by this act;

He may appeal to the court of general or quarter sessions having jurisdiction in the district; but no appeal is to be had in respect of any exercise of the discretion of the board in matters within their discretion.

A highway board may make the following improvements in the highways within their jurisdiction, and may, with the approval of the justices in general or quarter sessions assembled, borrow money for the purpose of defraying the expenses of such improvements :—

1. The conversion of any road that has not been stoned into a stoned road.

2. The widening of any road, the cutting off the corners in any road where land is required to be purchased for that purpose, the levelling roads, the making any new road, and the building or enlarging bridges.

3. The doing of any other work in respect of highways beyond ordinary repairs essential to placing any existing highway in a proper state of repair.

The acts of 1862 and 1864 are to be construed as one with the Highway Act, 1835, so far as is consistent with their provisions. Various points are specified in the 25 & 26 Vict. c. 61, s. 42, in reference to which the Highway Act, 1835, does not apply to the new districts. The most important one is the last.

The 39th, 40th, 43rd, 44th, and 45th sections of the principal act* relating to the accounts of surveyors shall not apply to the highway board of any district formed under this act.

CHAPTER XIV.

OF TRAMWAYS.

THERE is now in many—and in a constantly increasing number of—parishes, a new kind of way, which comes more or less under the control of the local—which may in some cases be a parochial—authority. We allude, of course, to Tramways. The power to construct tramways is regulated by an act passed in 1870 (33 & 34 Vict. c. 78), and although it would be foreign to our purpose to attempt anything like an analysis of its numerous and complicated clauses, it is necessary that we should indicate the relation in which the tramway system stands to the local government of the country. The subject, it is almost unnecessary. to say, is one of great and growing importance, and therefore

* The Act of 1835.

even the comparatively slight sketch of the legislation on the subject which our space permits us, will probably be both acceptable and useful to many of our readers.

Tramways are laid down in the public streets and highways under the authority of Acts of Parliament founded upon and confirming provisional orders of the Board of Trade.

The first stage in the process is to obtain the provisional order of the Board of Trade. As a preliminary to the application for such an order, the promoters of the tramway are required to give certain notices, and deposit their plans in the manner provided for by the act.

Provisional orders authorizing the construction of tramways in any district may be obtained by—

(1.) The local authority * of such district; or by—

---

* The following are the "local authorities" in the various districts enumerated :—

The City of London and the liberties thereof.—The Mayor, Aldermen, and Commons of the City of London ;

The Metropolis (1).—The Metropolitan Board of Works ;

Boroughs.—The mayor, aldermen, and burgesses, acting by the council ;

Any place not included in the above descriptions, and under the jurisdiction of commissioners, trustees, or other persons entrusted by any Local Act with powers of improving, cleansing, or paving any town.—The commissioners, trustees, or other persons entrusted by the Local Act with powers of improving, cleansing, or paving the town ;

Any place not included in the above descriptions, and within the jurisdiction of local board constituted in pursuance of the Public Health Act, 1848, and the Local Government Act, 1858, or one of such Acts.—The local board ;

Any place or parish not within the above descriptions, and in

(2.) Any person, persons, corporation, or company,
with the consent of the local authority of such
district; or of the road authority of such
district where such district is, or forms part of,
a highway district formed under the provisions
of the Highway Acts.

The approval of any intended application for a
provisional order by a local authority must be in
manner following :—

(1.) A resolution approving of the intention to
make such application must be passed at a
special meeting of the members constituting
such local authority.

(2.) Such special meeting must not be held unless a
month's previous notice of the same, and of the
purpose thereof, has been given in the manner
in which notices of meetings of such local
authority are usually given; and

(3.) Such resolutions must not be passed unless
two-thirds of the members constituting such
local authority are present and vote at such
special meeting, and a majority of those present
and voting concur in the resolution.

Supposing that a proposed tramway lies entirely

which a rate is levied for the maintenance of the poor.—The
vestry, select vestry, or other body of persons, acting by
virtue of any Act of Parliament, prescription, custom, or
otherwise, as or instead of a vestry or select vestry.

Where in any district there is a road authority distinct from
the local authority, the consent of such road authority shall
also be necessary in any case where power is sought to break
up any road subject to the jurisdiction of such road authority,
before any provisional order can be obtained.

within the jurisdiction of a single authority, that authority can impose an absolute veto upon its construction, by refusing its consent to the application for a provisional order. But when it is proposed to lay down a tramway in two or more districts, and any local or road authority having jurisdiction in any of such districts does not consent, the Board of Trade may, nevertheless, make a provisional order authorizing the construction of the tramway, if they are satisfied, after inquiry, that two-thirds of its length is proposed to be laid in a district or in districts the local and road authorities of which consent.

If the Board of Trade are satisfied that it is desirable to construct the proposed tramway—and for the purpose of arriving at a conclusion on the subject, they may, if they think fit, direct an inquiry in the districts to which it relates—they make a provisional order for its construction on the terms prescribed by the act. Thereupon the promoters have to deposit 4 per cent. on the amount of their estimate of the cost of the tramway, and to advertise the granting of the provisional order. The order will, however, not take effect until it is confirmed by an Act of Parliament, which will be introduced by the Board of Trade, but against which the opponents of any tramway may, if they desire, be heard by a select committee in either House of Parliament.

If the promoters, empowered by any provisional order to make a tramway, do not, within two years from the date of the same, or within any shorter period prescribed therein, complete the tramway and open it for public traffic; or,

If within one year from the date of the provisional
order, or within such shorter time as is prescribed
in the same, the works are not substantially commenced; or,

If the works having been commenced are suspended,
without a reason sufficient, in the opinion of the
Board of Trade, to warrant such suspension;

the powers given by the provisional order to the promoters for constructing such tramway cease to be
exercised, except as to so much of the same as is
then completed, unless the time be prolonged by the
special direction of the Board of Trade.

When a tramway has been completed, under the
authority of a provisional order, by any local authority,
or where any local authority has, under the provisions
of this act, acquired possession of a tramway, such
authority may, with the consent of the Board of
Trade, by lease, to be approved of by them, demise to
any person, persons, corporation, or company, the
right of user of the tramway, and taking in respect of
the same the tolls and charges authorized; or such
authority may leave the tramway open to be used by
the public, on payment of toll. But the local authority may not place or run carriages upon the tramway,
or demand and take tolls in respect of the use of such
carriages.

The promoters, for the purpose of making, forming,
laying down, maintaining, and renewing any tramway
duly authorized, may open and break up any road,
subject to the following regulations :—

(1.) They must give the road authority notice of
their intention, specifying the time at which

they will begin to do so, and the portion of
road proposed to be opened or broken up, such
notice to be given seven days at least before the
commencement of the work :

(2.) They must not open, or break up, or alter the
level of any road, except under the superintendence and to the reasonable satisfaction of
the road authority, unless that authority refuses
or neglects to give such superintendence at the
time specified in the notice, or discontinues the
same during the work :

(3.) They must pay all reasonable expenses to which
the road authority is put on account of such
superintendence :

(4.) They must not, without the consent of the road
authority, open or break up at any one time a
greater length than one hundred yards of any
road which does not exceed a quarter of a mile in
length, and in the case of any road exceeding a
quarter of a mile in length, the promoters shall
leave an interval of at least a quarter of a mile
between any two places at which they may open
or break up the road, and they shall not open
or break up at any such place a greater length
than one hundred yards.

When the promoters have opened or broken up any
portion of any road, they are under the following
further obligations :—

(1.) They must with all convenient speed, and in all
cases within four weeks at the most (unless the
road authority otherwise consents in writing),
complete the work on account of which they

opened or broke up the same, and (subject to
the formation, maintenance, or renewal of the
tramway) fill in the ground and make good the
surface, and, to the satisfaction of the road
authority, restore the portion of the road to as
good condition as that in which it was before it
was opened or broken up, and clear away all
surplus paving or metalling material, or rubbish
occasioned thereby :

(2.) They must in the meantime cause the place
where the road is opened or broken up to be
fenced and watched, and to be properly lighted
at night :

(3.) They must pay all reasonable expenses of the
repair of the road for six months after the same
is restored, as far as those expenses are increased
by the opening or breaking up.

The promoters must, at their own expense, maintain
in good repair, with such materials and in such
manner as the road authority directs, so much of any
road whereon any tramway belonging to them is laid
as lies between the rails of the tramway and (where
two tramways are laid by the same promoters in any
road at a distance of not more than four feet from
each other) the portion of the road between the tramways, and in every case so much of the road as extends
eighteen inches beyond the rails of and on each side
of any such tramway.

Other clauses provide for the protection of the
sewers, drains, &c., of a district, and prescribe the
mode in which disputes between tramway companies
and the local or road authority are to be settled ; while

a variety of sections prescribe the mode in which the tramways are to be used, and anticipate, so far as may be, the contingencies which may arise in their working or on the failure of the promoters to carry out or to maintain their undertaking. For these, however, we must refer our readers to the act itself, as for the most part they have only an indirect connection with the local government of a district or parish.

CHAPTER XV.

THE WATCHING AND LIGHTING OF PARISHES.

THE watching and lighting of parishes may take place under the 3 & 4 Will. IV. c. 90, if this act is adopted by a parish in the manner we shall proceed to describe. If three or more ratepayers present a requisition in writing to the churchwardens * of any parish, the latter must, within ten days after its receipt, call a public meeting of the ratepayers of the parish to decide whether the act shall be adopted and carried into execution in the parish. Of this meeting not less than ten and not more than twenty-one days' notice is to be given from the receipt of the requisition, and the notices calling it are to be affixed on the principal outer door of every parish church or chapel situate within the parish, or on the usual place of affixing notices relating to the parochial affairs of any such parish.

The meeting, when assembled, may choose their own

* This includes any chapelwarden, overseer, or other person usually calling meetings on parochial business.

chairman, who is to decide on any question that may arise as to the qualification of any person claiming to vote, or as to the eligibility of any candidate proposed for any office under the act. The first subject to be entertained will, of course, be whether the act shall be adopted by the parish. If a majority of two-thirds of the ratepayers present decide that the provisions of the act shall be adopted, then such provisions are forthwith to come into operation, and a certain number (not more than twelve, nor less than three) of inspectors are to be elected to carry them out. The ratepayers of the parish are at this first meeting, or some adjournment thereof, and in every succeeding year at a meeting to be called for that purpose, to determine the total amount of money which the inspectors shall have power to levy in any one year to carry into effect the provisions of the act, such sum to be raised by a rate.* Any five rated inhabitants of the parish may, however, at the meeting called to decide as to the adoption of the act, or at any adjournment thereof which may take place, demand a poll of the ratepayers qualified to vote upon the question, whether the act and its provisions, or any part thereof, shall be adopted in the parish, and also as to the amount of money to be raised in the first year, and the number of inspectors to be appointed. At this poll, of which due notice must be given in the manner prescribed by the act, a clear majority of the ratepayers must vote, and of these two-thirds must vote in favour of the adoption of the act, either wholly or for the

* After the act has been adopted, a simple majority of the ratepayers may determine the amount to be raised in any one year.

purpose of watching or lighting alone, and of the propositions submitted to them with respect to the amount to be raised and the number of inspectors to be appointed, otherwise the act cannot be adopted.

Suppose the act to be adopted, and the other propositions to be affirmed by the requisite majority, notice thereof is to be given to the churchwardens in the same manner as is prescribed with reference to the publication of the notices calling the original meeting. And in such case the act is from thenceforth to take effect and come into operation in such parish. But the inhabitants at any meeting duly called may, at any time after the expiration of three years from the time when the provisions of the act have been adopted, determine that they shall cease to be acted upon after a day to be fixed at such meeting.

The inspectors, under whose direction the act is to be carried out, are to be elected in the manner prescribed in the 17th section of the act. "The churchwardens of any parish adopting the provisions of this act, are to call a meeting of the ratepayers of such parish, and each candidate (being a person who resides within such parish and has been assessed or charged by the last rate made for relief of the poor in respect of a dwelling-house or other tenement or premises of the annual value according to the said rate of £15 or more), is to be eligible to be elected an inspector for the purpose of the act, and is to be proposed at the meeting by some person duly qualified to vote thereat, and seconded by some person in like manner duly qualified." If more inspectors. are proposed than are to be elected, and a poll is demanded by ten persons

qualified to vote, it must be granted. One-third of
the inspectors, or as near as may be, are to go out of
office each year (being, however, eligible for re-election),
but should the number of inspectors at any time fall
below three, in consequence of death, or any casual
vacancy, any vacancy or vacancies is or are to be
forthwith filled up in the same manner as the regular
annual appointments are made.

Annual meetings of the ratepayers are to be held
for the purpose of auditing the accounts of the inspectors, and electing inspectors in room of those who
annually retire. And the inspectors are to meet on the
first Monday in every month, when any rated inhabitant may attend and prefer any complaint which he
may think proper to make relating to anything done in
pursuance of or under pretence of the provisions of the
act. Special meetings are also to be held on the
requisition of one inspector when only three are appointed; or of two when more than three have been
elected.

As soon as the inspectors have been elected, they, or
any two or more of them, may, from time to time,
issue an order under their hands to the overseers of the
poor of the parish, requiring them to levy the amount
named in such order. But the total amount of the
sum thus ordered to be levied must not exceed that
which has been agreed upon by the inhabitants of the
parish. It will of course be raised by a rate, to which
owners and occupiers of houses, buildings, and property (other than lands), are to be rated at and pay a
rate in the pound three times greater than that at
which the owners and occupiers of land are rated at,

and pay for the purposes of the act. The rates are to be recovered in case of non-payment by summary proceedings before the justices of the peace, in much the same way as the payment of poor rates is enforced.

Sections 39 to 43 of the act make provision for the appointment of watchmen, and their being furnished with arms, clothing, &c., which they are to deliver up on removal under a penalty of £20. They are to be sworn in and have the power of constables, and persons assaulting or resisting them are subjected to a penalty of 40s., on conviction before one justice. When, however, any efficient county or borough police is established for the county or borough in which a parish is included, these watchmen are to be discontinued. Other sections give the requisite powers for establishing gas-works, laying mains, erecting lamps, &c.; and also for the provision of fire-engines. They also enforce penalties for various offences. And the act further authorizes the inspectors to contract for works directed to be done by the act, to sue for breach of contract, or to compound with the contractor, and to purchase or rent ground, or buildings, for the purpose of the act.

Rates assessed upon this act, or orders made by the inspectors, may be appealed against to the quarter sessions.

Finally; not only may parishes adopt the act either as to lighting or as to watching; or both as to lighting and watching: but the act may be adopted either wholly, or in part, by the inhabitants of a district of the parish, its operation of course being in that case confined to such district.*

* In any district where the Public Health Act, 1848, is in

CHAPTER XVI.

OF THE REMOVAL OF NUISANCES.

As the Nuisances Removal Act for England, 1855,* and the subsequent acts on the same subject, passed in 1860 (23 & 24 Vict. c. 77, s. 2), in 1866 (29 & 30 Vict. c. 90), 1868 (31 & 32 Vict. c. 115), and 1870 (33 & 34 Vict. c. 53), are in certain cases to be enforced by parochial authorities, it is necessary to give a brief outline of their principal provisions. We shall, however, confine ourselves within as narrow limits as possible, since this subject belongs more properly to the sanitary legislature of the country.

The following bodies are respectively charged with the execution of these acts :—1. In any place within which the Public Health Act is or shall be in force, the local board of health. 2. In any other place wherein a town council exists (except the city of London and the liberties thereof, the city of Oxford, and the borough of Cambridge), the mayor, aldermen, and burgesses

force, or where the Local Government Act, 1858, is adopted, and in which the Watching and Lighting Act, 3 & 4 Wm. IV. c. 90, has been adopted, the said last-mentioned act shall be superseded by the Local Government Act, 1858 ; and all lamps, lamp-posts, gas-pipes, fire-engines, hose, and other property vested in the inspectors for the time being under the said act, shall in all existing districts under the Public Health Act, 1848, and elsewhere upon the adoption of the Local Government Act, 1858, vest in the local board (21 & 22 Vict. c. 98, s. 46).

* 18 & 19 Vict. c. 121.

by the council. 3. In the city of London and the
liberties thereof, the commissioners of sewers for the
time being. 4. In other parishes within the area comprised within the district of the Metropolis Local
Management Act, every vestry and district board under
the Act 18 & 19 Vict. c. 120, shall, within their respective parish or district, be the local authority for the
removal of nuisances. 5. In the city of Oxford, the
local board. 6. In the borough of Cambridge, the
Local Improvement Act Commissioners. 7. In any
place where there is no local board of health or council,
and where there are trustees or commissioners under
an improvement act, such trustees or commissioners.
8. In any place where there is no local board of
health, council, trustees, nor commissioners, if there
shall be a board of guardians of the poor for such
place, or for any parish or union within which such
place is situated, such board of guardians. 9. If
there be no such board of guardians, the overseers of
the poor for such place, or for the parish of which such
a place forms part.* 10. In any place where a high-

* This act must be read, so far as relates to extra-parochial
places, with the Act for the Relief of the Poor in Extra-parochial Places (20 Vict. c. 19). The latter act provides that,
after the 31st December, 1857, every place entered separately
in the report of the registrar-general on the last census (1851),
which now is, or is reputed to be, extra-parochial, and wherein
no rate is levied for the relief of the poor, shall, for all the
purposes of (amongst other things) the removal of nuisances
be deemed a parish for such purposes, and shall be designated
by the name which is assigned to it in such report. A place
so situated will, therefore, come within the definition of a
parish, and be liable to all the incidents of a parish in respect
of the removal of nuisances injurious to health.

way board or a nuisances removal committee chosen by the vestry was subsisting, and at the time of the passing of the act of 1860 (6th August), employed or joined with other local authorities in employing a sanitary inspector or inspectors, such highway board or nuisances removal committee may continue to act, and a like committee may be annually chosen by the vestry for such place, in the same manner as if the amending act (that of 1860) had not been passed. But in case in any year the nuisances removal committee be not chosen for such place in manner so provided, or if the highway board or committee fail for two months in any year to appoint or employ a sanitary inspector or inspectors, the authority of the highway board or committee shall cease, and no like committee shall be chosen for such place, and the same body or persons shall thenceforth be the head authority for the place as if no such highway board or committee had been appointed therein.

The local body, whatever it may be, which is charged with carrying out the act, may appoint a committee of their own body to receive notices, take proceedings, and in all or certain specified respects, excute the act. And such local authority or their committee may, in each particular case, by order in writing under the hand of the chairman of such body or committee, empower any officer or person to make complaints and take proceedings on their behalf. They are also empowered to appoint a paid sanitary inspector, whose duty it is to inspect the district with a view to the preservation or improvement of its sanitary condition, and especially to ascertain the existence of nuisances dangerous to health.

We need not here advert to the modes in which the expenses of the act are to be defrayed in those cases in which it is carried out by corporations, trustees, &c., as they do not in any sense belong to the domain of parish law. It will be sufficient to say, that in the cases where the administration is or may be parochial, the charges are to be thus met:—

1. Where a board of guardians for a union is the local authority for the whole of the union, the charges and expenses shall by defrayed by means of an addition to be made to the rate for the relief of the poor of the parish or parishes for which the expense has been incurred, and be raised and paid in like manner as money expended for the relief of the poor.

2. Where the board of guardians is the local authority for two or more places maintaining their own poor, but not for all the places in the union, the charges and expenses shall be paid out of the poor rates of the places for which the board is the local authority.

3. When the board of guardians for a union is, under the act, the local authority for a single place maintaining its own poor, and when the board of guardians for any such single place, or the overseers of any such place, or "the nuisances removal committee" combined or chosen as before mentioned, in any such place are, under the act, the local authority for such place, the charges and expenses shall be defrayed out of the rates for the relief of the poor thereof.

4. When the board of guardians of a union is, under the act, the local authority for part only of any place maintaining its own poor, together with the

whole of any other such place, or part of any other such place, the board shall apportion such charges and expenses between or among any or every such part, and any or every such place; and so much of such charges and expenses as may be apportioned to any or every such place, for the whole of which such board is the local authority, shall be defrayed out of the rates or funds applicable to the relief of the poor thereof.

5. So much of any such charges and expenses as may be apportioned to part of a place maintaining its own poor, and any such charges and expenses incurred by any board of guardians or overseers where such board or overseers are the local authority for part of any such place only, shall be defrayed by means of an addition to be made to the rate for the relief of the poor thereof, and be raised and paid in like manner as money expended for the relief of the poor.

The following are deemed to be "nuisances" under the act of 1855, and subject to removal :—

1. Any premises in such a state as to be a nuisance or injurious to health.

2. Any pool, ditch, gutter, watercourse, privy, urinal, cesspool, drain, or ashpit, so foul as to be a nuisance or injurious to health.

3. Any animal so kept as to be a nuisance or injurious to health.

4. Any accumulation or deposit which is a nuisance or injurious to health.

But the act expressly provides, that no such accumulation or deposit as shall be necessary for the effectual carrying on of any business or manufacture shall be punishable as a nuisance, when it is proved to the satisfaction of the justices that the accumulation or deposit has not been kept longer than is necessary for the purpose of such business or manufacture, and that the best available means have been taken for protecting the public from injury to health thereby.

Under the Sanitary Act, 1866 (29 & 30 Vict. c. 90), the following are also nuisances :—

1. Any house or part of a house so over-crowded as to be dangerous or prejudicial to the health of the inmates.

2. Any factory, workshop, or workplace not already under the operation of any general act for the regulation of factories or bakehouses, not kept in a cleanly state or not ventilated in such a manner as to render harmless, as far as practicable, any gases, vapours, dust, or other impurities generated in the course of the work carried on therein that are a nuisance, or injurious or dangerous to health, or so over-crowded while work is carried on as to be dangerous or prejudicial to the health of those employed therein.

3. Any fire-place or furnace which does not, as far as practicable, consume the smoke arising from the combustible used in such fireplace or furnace, and is used within the district of a nuisance authority for working engines by steam, or in any mill, factory, dye-house, brewery, bakehouse, or gaswork, or in any manufactory or trade process whatever.

4. Any chimney (not being the chimney of a private dwelling-house) sending forth black smoke in such quantity as to be a nuisance. Provided, however, that when a person is summoned before the justices in respect of the nuisance arising from a fireplace or furnace which does not consume the smoke arising

from the combustible used in such fireplace or furnace, the justices may hold that no nuisance is created
within the meaning of the act, and dismiss the complaint if they are satisfied that such fireplace or furnace is constructed in such a manner as to consume as
far as practicable, having regard to the nature of the
manufacture or trade, all smoke arising therefrom, and
that such fireplace or furnace has been carefully
attended to by the person having charge thereof.

Under the same act, if the nuisance authorities. are
of opinion, upon the certificate of any legally qualified
medical practitioner, that the cleansing or disinfecting
of any house or any articles therein would tend to
prevent or check infectious or contagious disease, it is
their duty (by notice in writing) to require the owner
or occupier of such house to cleanse and disinfect the
same. If the person to whom this notice is given
does not comply with it in the time specified, he will
be liable to a penalty of not less that one shilling, and
not more than ten shillings, for every day he is in
default; and moreover, the nuisance authorities are to
cause the house to be disinfected, and may recover the
expenses from the owner or occupier in a summary
manner by proceedings before the justices. If, however, the owner or occupier is, from poverty or otherwise, unable, in the opinion of the nuisance authorities,
to carry out their requirements, they may, with his
consent, but at their own expense, cleanse and disinfect
the house or any articles in it likely to retain infection.

And further, the nuisance authority may provide a
proper place, with all necessary apparatus and attendance, for the disinfection of woollen articles, clothing,

or bedding, which have become infected, and may cause articles brought for disinfection to be disinfected free of charge. They may provide carriages for the conveyance to hospitals of persons suffering from a contagious or infectious disease, and places for the reception of dead bodies. And in any city or town of more than 5,000 inhabitants, they may, by application to the local government board, obtain power for the regulation, inspection, cleansing, and ventilation of common lodging-houses.

The local authority cannot in general take any proceedings under the act until notice of the existence of a nuisance has been given to them by—1. Some person aggrieved thereby. 2. The sanitary inspector or any paid officer under the local authority. 3. Two or more inhabitant householders of the parish or place to which the notice relates. 4. The relieving officer of the union or parish. 5. Any constable, or any officer of the constabulary or police force of the district or place. 6. And in case the premises be a common lodging-house, any person appointed for the inspection of common lodging-houses.

The local authority by themselves or their officers have the power to enter upon any premises for three purposes :—

1. To make an inspection for the purpose of taking proceedings against any nuisance of which they have received notice as above.

2. To examine premises where nuisances exist, to ascertain the course of drains, and to execute or inspect works ordered by the justices to be done under the act.

3. To remove or abate a nuisance in case of non-compliance with, or infringement of, the order of justices, or to inspect or examine any carcase, meat, poultry, game, flesh, fish, fruit, vegetables, corn, bread, or flour, under the powers and for the purposes of the act.

When a nuisance has been ascertained to exist, the owner or occupier of the premises in which it has been found must, if he refuse to remove it, be summoned before any two justices of the peace in petty sessions or before a stipendiary magistrate, who, on proof of the existence of a nuisance, may by their order require the person on whom it is made :—

To provide sufficient privy accommodation, means of drainage or ventilation, or to make safe and habitable ;

Or to pave, cleanse, whitewash, disinfect, or purify the premises which are a nuisance or injurious to health, or such part thereof as the justices my direct in their order ;

Or to drain, empty, cleanse, fill up, amend, or remove the injurious pool, ditch, gutter, watercourse, privy, urinal, cesspool, drain, or ashpit which is a nuisance or injurious to health ;

Or to provide a substitute for that complained of ;

Or to carry away the accumulation or deposit which is a nuisance or injurious to health ;

Or to provide for the cleanly and wholesome keeping of the animal kept, so as not to be a nuisance or injurious to health ;

Or if it be proved to the justices to be impossible so to provide, then to remove the animal, or any or all of these things (according to the nature of the nuisance) ;

Or to do such other works or acts as are necessary to abate the nuisance complained of, in such manner, and within such time, as in such order shall be specified.

And if the justices are of opinion that such or the like nuisance is likely to recur, the justices may further prohibit the recurrence of it, and direct the works necessary to prevent such recurrence as the case may require.*

Any order may be enforced under a penalty upon delay; while, on the other hand, it is subject to an appeal to the quarter sessions.

If the owner or occupier of any premises does not comply with the order of the justices for the removal or abatement of a nuisance, the nuisance authority may do what is requisite, and charge the expense to the owner or occupier, as the case may be, and may recover the same by summary proceedings before the justices. In case the owner is liable, they may, under certain limitations, require the occupier to pay, leaving him to deduct the sum expended (as he is authorized to do) from the rent due to his landlord.†

The various acts we mentioned at the beginning of this chapter also give the local authority power, when necessary for the public health, to make new drains, sewers, and watercourses, and to defray their cost by assessing (but so that the amount in no case exceed a shilling in the pound on the assessment to the highway rate if any) every house, building, or premises then or at any time thereafter using the sewer, &c., to

* The justices may also prohibit the habitation of houses unfit for the purpose.

† See 29 & 30 Vict. c. 90, s. 34.

such payment "either immediate or annual, or distributed over a term of years, as they may think just
and reasonable."

Proceedings may be taken under this act (before
the justices or a stipendiary magistrate) against persons fouling water with gas washings; or exposing for
sale meat unfit for food; or carrying on noxious trades
or manufactures (not having used the best practicable
means for abating the nuisance or preventing or coun-
teracting the effluvia); or overcrowding a house containing more than one family.

The board of guardians for every union, or parish not
within a union, is * now the local authority for executing the Diseases Prevention Act, 1855, in every
place within their respective unions and parishes; and
in every parish or place in England, not within a
union, and for which there is no board of guardians,
the overseers of the poor are the local authority to
execute the act.

The expenses incurred in the execution of the
Diseases Prevention Act by the board of guardians for
a union are to be defrayed out of the common fund
thereof, and the expenses of the board of guardians or
overseers of the poor of any single parish or place are
to be defrayed out of the rates for the relief of the
poor of such parish or place.

The act in question is only to be put in force by an
Order in Council, when any part of England is
threatened with formidable epidemic, endemic, or
contagious disease. The Local government board are
then to issue directions and regulations :—1. For the

* By the 23 & 24 Vict. c. 77, s. 11.

speedy interment of the dead. 2. For house-to-house visitation. 3. For the dispensing of medicines. 4. Guarding against the spread of disease. 5. Affording to persons afflicted by, or threatened with, epidemic, endemic, or contagious diseases, such medical aid and such accommodations as may be required. And these directions and regulations are to be carried out and enforced by the boards of guardians and the overseers respectively.

CHAPTER XVII.

OF CHURCH RATES.

A CHURCH RATE is, at common law, a rate levied upon persons in respect of their occupation of land or houses in any parish, " for the necessary repairing and sustaining the fabric of the church, and of all public chapels within or adjoining thereto, and also of the ornaments thereof ; and for providing all things necessary for the proper celebration of divine service, and the administration of the sacraments thereof."* In order that a church rate should, at common law, be legal, it must be laid for one, or other, or all of these purposes, and for none other.

At common law, these were the only purposes for which a church rate could be imposed ; but, under the 58 Geo. III. c. 45, and the 59 Geo. III. c. 134, powers

* The payment of the incumbent's salary is not included in this, and if any part of the rate is intended to be applied thereto, the rate will be bad.

K

were given to raise money on the security of the rates
for enlarging and extending the accommodation in
existing churches, or repairing the same; and (as a
necessary means of doing so) to levy rates to pay the
interest and principal of such loans.

The Church Building Acts gave similar powers for
raising money to defray the cost of building new
churches. And, in addition to these measures, there
are in operation in different parts of the country,
local acts, under which church rates, or rates in
the nature of church rates, are levied for a variety of
purposes.

It is necessary to distinguish carefully between the
common law and the statutory church rates, because,
as we shall proceed to show, they are affected very
differently by the Compulsory Church Rates Abolition
Act, 1868.*

By that act, the compulsory levy of the common law
church rate was terminated, the first clause providing
that "from and after the passing of this act, no suit
shall be instituted or proceedings taken in any
ecclesiastical or other court, or before any justice or
magistrate, to enforce or compel the payment of any
church rate made in any parish or place in England
or Wales."

It was at the same time enacted, that "this act shall
not affect vestries on the making, assessing, or receiving,
or otherwise dealing with any church rate, save in so far
as relates to recovery thereof."

The effect of these two provisions taken together, is,
that while the old law remains theoretically in force,

* 31 & 32 Vict. c. 109.

so far as relates to the mode of sanctioning a rate by the vestry, as to the purposes to which the rate is to be applied, and as to the mode in which it is to be assessed, this law has now little or no practical value, except as a guide to the mode in which the churchwardens and vestry should conduct their business. It is, no doubt, true, that if an illegal rate were made, a parishioner might, as heretofore, question it in the ecclesiastical court. But then, as every one has now in his own hands the far simpler remedy of refusing to pay, it can scarcely be anticipated that any one will hereafter indulge in the idle luxury of instituting a suit for the purpose of establishing his own view of the manner in which a rate should be assessed or levied. Still, as the old law does subsist to the extent, and in the manner, we have described, and as it ought no doubt to guide and govern the action of the churchwardens in regard to the discharge of this part of their duties, a brief statement of its principle and provisions may still be found useful.

In order that a church rate should be valid, it must be voted by a majority of the parishioners present at a vestry meeting duly convened by the churchwardens, by a notice stating the object of such meeting. The rate will be void if an insufficient notice of the meeting * be given; or if it be laid against the will of the majority of the parishioners present at the vestry.† If, indeed, no parishioners are present at the vestry

* As to notice, see Chapter VII., on Vestries.

† This latter point was established, after protracted legal controversy, in the famous Braintree case, reported as *Gosling* v. *Veley*, 4 House of Lords Cases, 679.

meeting, then it is said that the churchwardens may make a rate by their own authority.

A church rate ought to be laid before the expenses which it is intended to defray are incurred; for the parishioners have a right to consider and determine upon their necessity or propriety. And if the rate be made to reimburse the churchwardens for any expenses, *except those incurred in the current year,* it will be invalid. Even if any part of the rate be laid to cover a retrospective payment, the whole will be bad. And although the vestry authorizes expenses before they are incurred, a retrospective rate to defray them will be equally invalid.

Church rates are assessed, like other rates, upon the rent of land and houses, and are payable by the occupiers thereof, whether they are resident in the parish or not. Unless, also, there is a usage to the contrary, stock-in-trade is rateable to the church rates. The glebe or endowments of the parish church are, indeed, exempt from rating; but lands belonging to the church of a foreign parish are liable in the same manner as other property.

Church rates (*i.e.* of course of the common law or ordinary kind) being now reduced to the level of a voluntary impost, which any one may pay or not, just as he pleases, it became not only harmless, but expedient, to extend somewhat the powers of self taxation possessed by members of the establishment. Accordingly, it is provided by the sixth section of the Compulsory Church Rates Abolition Act, that whenever any ecclesiastical district, having within its limits a consecrated church in use for the purposes of divine worship, has been legally constituted out of any parish or parishes, the inhabitants shall not be entitled to vote for or in reference to a church rate or the expenditure thereof at any vestry meeting of the parish or parishes out of which the said district was formed, nor shall they be assessed to any rate made in relation to the parish church of such parish or parishes, but they may assemble in vestry, and make a rate in relation to the church of their own district in like manner as if such church were the church of an ancient parish. Nothing, however, in this act is to affect any right of burial to which the inhabitants of the district may be entitled in the churchyard of the mother church.

Although they are not compellable, it is nevertheless lawful, for all bodies corporate, trustees, guardians, and committees (*i.e.* of lunatics) who or whose cestuisque trust are in the occupation of any lands, houses, or tenements, to pay any church rate made in respect of such property, and such payment is to be allowed them in any accounts rendered by them respectively.*

Then, by sect. 8 of the same act, "no person who makes default in paying the amount of a church rate for which he is rated, shall be entitled to inquire into, or object to, or vote in respect of the expenditure of the moneys arising from such church rate; and if the occupier of any premises shall make default for one month after demand in payment of any church rate for which he is rated, the owner shall be entitled to pay the same, and shall thereupon be entitled, until the next succeeding church rate is made, to stand for

* 31 & 32 Vict. c. 109, sec. 7.

all purposes relating to church rates (including the
attending at vestries and voting thereat) in the place
in which such occupier would have stood."

We have now to deal with statutory church rates,
that is to say, with rates levied under particular Acts
of Parliament, either public or private, for special purposes, or in fulfilment of contracts, or for the repayment of money advanced upon their security. If the
rate, although called a church rate, is, in fact, applied
to secular purposes, no religious body can possibly
entertain any conscientious reluctance to it; while
the payment of rates on which loans have been raised,
could not, without great injustice to those to whom
the faith of parliament was pledged, have been
rendered less imperative than formerly. The Compulsory Church Rates Act has, therefore, expressly maintained in full force and vigour the different classes of
rates to which we have just referred.

The second section provides, that "when, in pursuance
of any general or local act, any rate may be made and
levied which is applicable partly to ecclesiastical purposes and partly to other purposes, such rate shall be
made and levied, and applied, for such last-mentioned
purposes only, and so far as it is applicable to such
purposes shall be deemed to be a separate rate, and
not a church rate, and shall not be affected by
this act." Then, on the other hand, it enacts that
"where in pursuance of any Act of Parliament a
mixed fund, arising partly from rates affected by
this act and partly from other sources, is directed to be
applied to purposes some of which are ecclesiastical
purposes, the portion of such fund which is derived

from such other sources shall be henceforth primarily applicable to such of the said purposes as are ecclesiastical."

Then by clause 3, " in any parish where a sum of money is at the time of the passing of this act due on the security of church rates, or of rates in the nature of church rates, to be made or levied in such parish under the provisions of any Act of Parliament, or where any money in the name of church rate is ordered to be raised under any such provisions, such rates may still be made and levied, and the payment thereof enforced by process of law, pursuant to such provisions, for the purpose of paying off the money so due, or paying the money so ordered to be raised, and the costs incidental thereto, but not otherwise, until the same shall have been liquidated : Provided, that the accounts of the churchwardens of such parish in reference to the receipt and expenditure of the moneys levied under such acts shall be audited annually by the auditor of the Poor Law Union within whose district such parish. shall be situate, unless another mode of audit is provided by Act of Parliament." The fourth clause declares, that " this act shall not affect any enactment in any private or local Act of Parliament under the authority of which church rates may be made or levied in lieu of or in consideration of the extinguishment or of the appropriation to any other purpose of any tithes, customary payments, or other property or charge upon property, which tithes, payments, property, or charge, previously to the passing of such act, had been appropriated by law to ecclesiastical purposes as defined by this act, or in consideration of the abolition of tithes in any place, or upon any contract made, or for good or valuable consideration given, and every such enactment shall continue in force in the same manner as if this act had not passed."

The courts of law never would grant a mandamus to compel the laying of an ordinary church rate; and it is therefore almost unnecessary to say that they will not do so now, when the payment of the rate is perfectly optional with the parishioners. But the case of church rates levied for the repayment of principal and interest, when money has been borrowed, under thè 59 Geo. III. c. 34, to rebuild 'a church, stands on quite a different footing. Then there is a statutory obligation, which is just as binding as any other obligation of the same kind; and accordingly, with respect to such a rate, a mandamus will be issued, directed to the churchwardens and directing them to lay and levy such a rate in accordance with the terms of the act, and in fulfilment of their predecessors' contract.

CHAPTER XVIII.

OF COUNTY AND BOROUGH RATES.

As the county and borough rates are levied by means of thę parochial machinery, it is necessary briefly to state here the law applicable to their assessment.

The county rate is raised for, and applied to, the following purposes:—Repairing county bridges, and highways adjoining; the removal of prisoners for transportation; carrying prisoners to gaol; allowance

to discharge prisoners ; building and repairing houses
of correction and shire halls; salary of chaplains and
officers, and setting prisoners to work ; expenses relating to insolvents, court houses, &c. ; providing
county lunatic asylums ; fees of gaolers, and other
officers ; burying dead bodies cast on shore ; expenses
of prosecutions; treasurer's salary; prosecuting vagrants, &c. ; procuring copies of the imperial standards
of weights and measures; militia charges; and the
payment of half the expense of prosecuting masters
for ill-treating their parish apprentices.*

By the 15 & 16 Vict. c. 81, which now regulates
the assessment of this rate, the quarter sessions of
every county are, from time to time, to accept a committee of justices to prepare a basis † or standard for
fair and equal county rates, which is to be founded
and prepared rateably and equally according to the full
and fair annual value of the property rateable to the
relief of the poor in each parish or extra-parochial
place. In order to the preparation of this basis, the
committee may direct the overseers, constables, assessors, and collectors of public rates, for any parish, &c.,
and all others having the custody or management of
any public or parochial rates or valuations of such
parish, &c., to make returns of the full and fair *net*
annual value of the whole or any part of the property
within the parish, &c., liable to be assessed to the

* Steer's Parish Law, by Hodgson, p. 453.
† The "basis" is a statement of the rateable value of the
property in each parish. The county rate is, as we shall see
presently, charged upon each parish in proportion to the value
of the property therein contained.

county rate, with the date of the last valuation for the assessment of such parish, &c. The overseers, &c., are to lay their returns before the vestry, or other meeting of the inhabitants, at which the public business of the parish, &c., is commonly transacted, before presenting them to the committee. The latter have the power to call upon the overseers, &c., to produce all documents relating to the assessment of the property in the several parishes, and also to be examined on oath touching the same. Whenever the committee alter the basis of assessment, copies thereof are to be printed, and to be sent to all the justices, and to the overseers, constables, &c., in each parish. And when a basis has been adopted by the committee, it has to be confirmed by the quarter sessions, who may then entertain any appeal lodged against it on the part of any parish, on the ground that it is rated too high, or that other parishes are rated too low. The "basis" having been confirmed, the justices, at general or quarter sessions, or at any adjournment thereof, may, whenever circumstances appear to require it, order a fair and equal county rate to be made, for all purposes to which such rate is liable, according to the basis in force for the time being; and may assess every parish, &c., within the limits of their commissions, rateably and equally, according to a pound rate to be fixed by such justices upon the said basis, upon the full annual value of the property, &c., rateable to the relief of the poor. Appeals may be made against the rate on the part of any parish, on the grounds stated in section 22 of the above statute.

Subject to such appeals, the sessions are to send a

printed list of the parishes, &c., assessed to the rate, and the rateable value upon which each is assessed, to the overseers, constables, or others, charged with the collection of the county rate; and to send precepts to the guardians of unions or single parishes, stating the sum assessed for each rate on each parish in the union, and requiring them to cause the aggregate of such sums to be paid out of the money held on behalf of each parish to the county treasurer. The guardians are to raise the money in the same manner as poor rates, and to pay it as required by the precepts. Should the guardians disobey their precepts, then the justices may, by warrants, direct the overseers, petty constables, &c., of each parish to collect and pay to the county treasurer the sum charged on the parish, with an addition of 10 per cent., which is to be applied to the same purposes as the county rate.

Boroughs having quarter sessions of their own are, by the 12 & 13 Vict. c. 82, relieved, under certain circumstances, from paying their quota to the county rate for the support of gaols, houses of correction, and lunatic asylums.

Unless they are authorized so to do by special acts of parliament, the justices have no right to lay a county rate to pay a debt incurred for county purposes. In all these cases, the principle is, that those who are liable to a rate at the time an expense is incurred are the proper and only parties to pay it.

BOROUGH RATE.

This is a rate originally levied only in boroughs, scheduled in the Municipal Corporations Act (1835), although, as we shall presently see, subsequently extended to other boroughs. By the Act just mentioned (5 & 6 Wm. IV. c. 76, s. 92), the annual proceeds of all the corporate property, and all fines and penalties for offences against the act, are to be carried to the "borough fund;" and should that fund be inadequate to defray the corporate expenses, the council are empowered to levy a borough rate to meet the deficiency. Then, by 1 Vict. c. 81, s. 1, they may order the churchwardens and overseers to pay the amount of the rate for which a parish is liable out of the poor rate, or to make and collect a pound rate for the amount; and on refusal or neglect to do so, the amount may be levied on their goods by distress, by warrant under the hand and seal of the mayor or two justices for the borough; and if any person refuse to pay the said pound rate, the amount may be levied on his goods in the same manner.

This rate is extended to boroughs other than corporate by the 17 & 18 Vict. c. 71, by which it is enacted that the justices of any borough, not being within the Municipal Corporations Act, and not being liable to contribute to the county rate may make a borough rate, in the nature of a county rate, for defraying any expenses incurred before 31st July, 1854, and which are thereafter to be incurred, for all or any of the purposes defined in the Municipal Corporations Act, 1835, as purposes for which a borough rate may be levied; and they, and all persons acting under their authority, are to have, within the borough, all powers and protection given to justices by the 55 Geo. III. c. 51, and to town councils by any acts relating to the making of

borough rates.   There is an appeal against such a rate
to the recorder of the borough, or in the absence of
such a functionary, to the quarter sessions of the county.

CHAPTER XIX.

OF POOR RATES.

THE present system of rating for the relief of the
poor is based upon the act 43 Elizabeth, c. 2, s. 1,
which enacts "that the churchwardens and overseers
of the poor of every parish, or the greater part of
them, shall, by and with the consent of two or more
justices of the same county, whereof one to be of the
quorum, dwelling in or near the same parish or division where the same parish doth lie, raise weekly or
otherwise, by taxation of every inhabitant, parson,
vicar and other, and of every occupier of lands,
houses, tithes impropriate, propriations of tithes, coal-
mines, or saleable underwoods in the said parish, in
such competent sum and sums of money as they shall
think fit, a convenient stock of flax, hemp, wool,
thread, iron, and other necessary ware and stuff, to set
the poor on work; and also competent sums of money
for and towards the necessary relief of the lame, impotent, old, and blind, and such other amongst them
being poor and not able to work; and also for the
putting out of such children to be apprentices—to be
gathered out of the same parish according to the
ability of the same parish, and to do and execute all
other things as well for the disposing of the said stock

or otherwise concerning the premises, as to them shall seem convenient."

Such were the terms in which was couched the first effective provision of a fund for the relief of the poor, and although some of the provisions of this enactment have grown obsolete, it still in principle regulates the imposition of the poor rate. This rate can still only be levied by the churchwardens and overseers, or the major part of them, of every parish, or of every village and township in cases were separate overseers are appointed for such village and township. Upon them the duty of levying it is cast, and if they neglect it, its fulfilment may be enforced by mandamus, or they may be indicted.

As we have already seen, the act 43 Elizabeth requires the rate to be confirmed or allowed by two or more justices, dwelling in or near the parish, &c. The justices, however, have no power to refuse the allowance of a rate. But after this purely ministerial act on their part has been performed, the rate must not be altered, even with the magistrate's approval, by inserting the names of additional ratepayers, or varying the sums at which they are rated. But by 54 Geo. III. c. 170, s. 11, "two or more justices in petty sessions may, upon application, and with the consent of the overseers or other parish officers, and on proof of the party's inability from poverty to pay such rate, excuse the payment and strike out the name of such party from the rate."

Public notice of the rate must be given by the overseers on the next Sunday after it has been allowed by the justices. If this be omitted, the rate is *null and void;* and the only legal mode of doing this is by affixing the notice, previously to divine service, on or near to the principal doors of all the churches and chapels within the parish or place for which the rate is made. The inhabitants may subsequently inspect the rate at all reasonable times.* And any person rated, may at all reasonable times take copies or extracts from the rate, without paying anything for the same.†

The poor rate can only be made nominally for the relief of the poor; but different acts of parliament have authorized various payments to be made out of it, most of which will be found noticed under the various chapters of this work, to which their consideration naturally belongs.

The 43 Elizabeth authorizes the levy of a poor rate upon both *inhabitants* and *occupiers* of land in the parish. As, however, an act is now and has been for some time annually passed, exempting inhabitants from rating in respect of profits derived from stock-in trade, or other property, the practical result is, that only occupiers of land or houses are now rated. The only exception to this is, that the parson and vicar are liable to be rated for their tithes in the parish.

The rate is then imposed upon each occupier in reference to an estimate of, and in proportion to, the net annual value of the lands, houses, &c., which he may occupy, that is to say, of the rent at which the same might be reasonably expected to let from year to year, free of all the usual tenant's rates and taxes and tithe commutation rent charge (if any), and deducting

* 17 Geo. II. c. 3, s. 2. † 6 & 7 Wm. IV. c. £0, s. £.

therefrom the probable annual average cost of the repairs, insurance, and other expenses (if any) necessary to maintain them in a state to command such rent. The poor-law commissioners, or the guardians of the poor (on the application of the majority of the overseers of any parish), may order a survey and new valuation of the property in the parish if they think fit.*

All persons must be rated on the same scale, that is to say, one must not be rated at rack rent, another at three-fourths the value, and so on. If this is not so, any party rated may appeal to the quarter sessions and have the rate quashed.

The rate should be prospective, *i. e.,* to meet the estimated expenses of a forthcoming period, which may be one of a quarter or half a year. One set of church-wardens or overseers cannot, it seems clear, lay a rate to reimburse their predecessors in office, except for expenses incurred in the relief of the poor during such period as they were unable to collect a rate which they had laid, on account of an appeal having been lodged against it.

In order to render a person liable to be rated to the poor, he must be the " beneficial occupier " of lands

* With respect to the mode in which, and the persons by whom, the valuation here spoken of is to be made, see the chapter— *Of Parochial Assessment.* These matters are now regulated by the 25 & 26 Vict. c. 103, the 27 & 28 Vict. c. 39, the 31 & 32 Vict. c. 122, and the 32 & 33 Vict. c. 67. The principles of rating, the law as to appeals against rates, and other points noticed in the present chapter, are not affected by those acts which are entirely confined to the subject of valuation.

or houses in the parish, *i.e.*, his occupation must be
capable of yielding him a profit. Servants in possession
of premises are not therefore rateable; and it was
formerly supposed that the persons who erect, or the
trustees or governors of an hospital, almshouse, or
other charitable institution, were also exempt, seeing
that they do not derive any personal benefit from their
occupation. It has, however, been decided by the
House of Lords (*Jones* v. *The Mersey Dock and
Harbour Company*, 11 House of Lords Cases, 443), that
trustees who are in law the tenants and occupiers of
valuable property upon trust for public and even charitable purposes, such as hospitals and lunatic asylums,
are rateable, if the property yields, or is capable of
yielding, a net annual value; that is to say, a clear rent
over and above the probable average annual cost of the
repairs, insurance, and other expenses (if any) necessary
to maintain the property in a state to command such
rent. An officer of such an institution has always been
held rateable in respect of a house or rooms appropriated to his own use. Court-houses, gaols, churches,
chapels (whether belonging to the Established Church
or to Dissenters); lands or houses in the possession of
the Crown or the public; lands used for a public purpose;
"land, houses, or building belonging to any society instituted for the purposes of science, literature, or the fine
arts exclusively, either as tenant or owner, and occupied
by it for the transaction of its business, and for carrying into effect its purposes,"*—are all exempt from

* In order to entitle a society to this exemption, the promo-
tion of science, literature, or the fine arts must be its primary
object, and not merely the gratification of its members by

L

liability to be assessed to the poor rate. Workhouses are rateable to the parish in which they are situate.

In addition to the cases of absolute exemption from assessment to the poor rate, there is one instance in which such exemption is optional with the local authority. By the 32 & 33 Vict. c. 40, every authority having power to impose or levy any rate upon the occupier of any building or part of a building used exclusively as a Sunday school, or Ragged school, may exempt such building, or part of a building, from any rate for any purpose whatever which such authority has power to impose or levy.*

A rate on a foreign ambassador cannot be levied by dirtress, nor can any of his suite be rated, if they be clearly within the meaning of the statute, 7 Anne, c. 12.†

means of such pursuits. There must be an express rule of the society prohibiting any dividend amongst its members. And it must have obtained the certificate of the barrister appointed to certify friendly societies.—*Steer's Parish Law, by Hodgson*, pp. 482–3.

* A Sunday-school is defined by the act to mean "any school used for giving religious education gratuitously to children and young persons on Sunday, and on work days for the holding of classes and meetings in furtherance of the same object, and without pecuniary profit being derived therefrom." A ragged school means "any school for the gratuitous education of children and young persons of the poorest class, and for the holding of classes and meetings in furtherance of the same object, and without any pecuniary benefit being derived therefrom, except to the teacher or teachers employed."

† But when this privilege was claimed by a servant of an ambassador whose goods had been distrained for a poor rate, he being the tenant of the house, part of which he let out in lodgings, and a teacher of languages, and also prompter at the

It would be utterly impossible here to attempt the merest outline of the principles which the courts have laid down as those upon which the various kinds of real property are to be rated. The mode in which the net annual value of the occupation of canals, docks, water and gas works, tithes, mines, quarries, saleable underwood, &c., is to be estimated for the purpose of rating, has in each case given rise to abundant litigation, and has in each case been more or less clearly and conclusively settled at the expense of a succession of litigants. But we cannot deal with these points in the space at our command. The attempt would, moreover, be utterly unprofitable, as when any disputes arise with respect to them, recourse must necessarily be had to professional assistance.

Although, as a general rule, the occupant of property is liable to the poor rate, a very important exception is made in the case of *small tenements* let for short terms. The mode in which they are or may be rated under an act passed in 1869 is a matter of so much importance to the interior economy of a parish, that we have devoted a separate chapter to the subject (see Chapter XX, p. 149).

The appeals against poor rates are in some cases specially provided for by local acts. We here deal only with the general law of the land upon this subject.

By the 6 & 7 Will. IV. c. 96, s. 6, the justices acting for every petty sessional division are, four times a year at least, to hold a special sessions (of which

opera-house, it was said by the Court that such a privilege as this, or the like case, would be absurd, and not at all within the principle upon which the right of ambassadors was founded.

they must give twenty-eight days' notice) for hearing
appeals against rates. At such sessions they are to
hear and determine upon all objections to any rate on
account of inequality, unfairness, or incorrectness in
the valuation of the property included therein. Their
power of inquiry does not extend to the liability of any
property to be rated, but only as to its true value and
the fairness of the amount at which it has been rated.
They may, upon hearing the appeal,—1. Dismiss it;
2. Amend the rate; or, 3. Quash the rate. And their
decision is final unless the party dissatisfied with it
gives notice within fourteen days of his intention to
appeal to the quarter sessions. This latter and higher
court has power to entertain a greater range of objections to the rate than falls within the cognizance of
the inferior tribunal. A rate may be appealed against
to the quarter sessions on the ground :—1. That the
appellant should not have been rated at all. 2. That
the rate is unequal, by reason of the appellant being
overrated; of other persons being underrated; or of
other persons not being rated at all. 3. That the rate
is bad on the face of it, *i. e.*, that it is not made in the
form required by statute. 4. That the rate is not
made by proper persons. 5. That the rate is not made
for a proper purpose. 6. That the rate is not made
for a proper period.

If the appellant prove his case, the sessions may
either amend the rate so as to do him justice; or if
the objection to the rate cannot be thus removed, they
may quash it altogether.

The payment of poor rates is enforced by summon-
ing the party from whom they are due before two

justices, who, if satisfied of his liability, will issue
a warrant of distress against his goods, both for the
amount of the rates and the cost of the summons and
distress.*

They may also order the person to be imprisoned for
three months in default of distress. But if, before
imprisonment, he tender payment of rates and costs,
the proceedings are to be stayed.

If the sessions quash any rate, it is nevertheless
(*unless the sessions make an order to the contrary, either
as to the whole or part*) to be levied as if there had
been no appeal; and the sums collected or recovered
are to be taken on account of the next good rate for
the same parish.

No action can be brought against the justices who
issue a distress warrant on the ground of any defect or
irregularity in the rate, or of the party upon whose
goods it is executed not being liable to its payment.
But those who execute a warrant my be sued as
trespassers, if in so doing they are guilty of illegal
violence.

CHAPTER XX.

OF THE RATING OF TENEMENTS LET FOR SHORT TERMS, AND OF SMALL TENEMENTS.

WE mentioned, in the course of the previous chapter,
that poor rates are, as a rule, assessed upon, and

* The warrant authorizes the seizure of his goods at any
place in the same county. If sufficient distress cannot be
found there, and if he have any property in another county, a
warrant may be obtained for its seizure from the justices
thereof.

payable by, the occupier, but that there was, or might be, an exception in the case of small tenements or tenements let for short terms. It now becomes our duty to state the law relating to the rating of this class of property, which is embodied in an act (32 & 33 Vict. c. 41) passed in 1869.

The first clause of that act provides, that "the occupier of any rateable hereditament, let to him for a term not exceeding three months, may deduct the amount paid by him in respect of any poor rate assessed upon such hereditament from the rent due, or accruing due, to the owner; and that every such payment shall be a valid discharge of the rent to the extent of the rate so paid." The second clause, at the same time provides, that "no such occupier shall be compelled to pay to the overseers at one time, or within four weeks, a greater amount of the rate than would be due for one quarter of the year."

So far, the operation of the act extends only to the relief of the occupier, without in any way altering the incidence of the rate. The following clauses deal with the larger question of composition for rates, and, as it will be seen, revive, in a somewhat modified form, that "compound householder" who was so summarily abolished by the Reform Act of 1867.

In case the rateable value of any hereditament does not exceed £20, if the hereditament is situate in the metropolis, or £13 if situate in any parish wholly or partly within the borough of Liverpool, or £10 if situate in any parish wholly or partly within the city of Manchester or the borough of Birmingham, or £8 if situate elsewhere, and the owner of such hereditament is willing to enter into an agreement, in writing, with the overseers to become liable to them for the poor rates assessed in respect of such hereditament for any term, not being less than one year, from the date of such agreement, and to pay the poor rates whether the hereditament is occupied or not, the overseers may, subject, nevertheless, to the control of the vestry, agree with the owner to receive the rates from him, and to allow to him a commission not exceeding 25 per cent. on the amount thereof.*

Under the clause we have just cited, the arrangement contemplated between the owner and the overseers is one of a purely voluntary character. It rests entirely with the owner whether he will, or will not, undertake to pay the rates falling due in respect of his property. But under the following section (4) :—

"The vestry of any parish may, from time to time, *order* that the owners of all rateable hereditaments to which section 3 of this act extends, situate within such parish, shall be rated to the poor rate in respect of such rateable hereditaments, instead of the occupiers, on all rates made after the date of such order ; and thereupon, and so long as such order shall be in force, the following enactments shall have effect :—

" 1. The overseers shall rate the owners instead of the occupiers, and shall allow to them an abatement or deduction of 15 per cent. from the amount of the rate.

" 2. If the owner of one or more such rateable hereditaments shall give notice to the overseers, in writing, that he is willing to be rated for

* Sec. 3.

any term, not being less than one year, in
respect of all such rateable hereditaments of
which he is the owner, whether the same be
occupied or not, the overseers shall rate such
owner accordingly, and allow to him a further
abatement or deduction, not exceeding 15 per
cent. from the amount of the rate during the
time he is so rated.

" 3. The vestry may, by resolution, rescind any
such order after a day to be fixed by them,
such day being not less than six months after
the passing of such resolution; but the order
shall continue in force with respect to all rates
made before the date on which the resolution
takes effect.

" Provided that this clause shall not be applicable to
any rateable hereditament in which a dwelling-house
shall not be included."

If an owner who has become liable to pay the poor
rate, omits or neglects to pay before the 5th day of
June in any year, any rate, or any instalment thereof,
which has become due previously to the preceding 5th
day of January, and has been duly demanded by a
demand-note delivered to him, or left at his usual
or last-known place of abode, he will not be entitled
to deduct or receive any commission, abatement, or
allowance to which he would (except for such omission
or neglect) be entitled under this act, but will be
liable to pay, and " shall pay," such rate or instalment
in full.*

Where an owner who has undertaken, whether by

* Sec. 5.

agreement with the occupier or with the overseers, to pay the poor rates, or has otherwise become liable to pay the same, omits or neglects to pay any such rate, the occupier may pay the same, and deduct the amount from the rent due, or accruing due, to the owner; and the receipt for such rate will be a valid discharge of the rent to the extent of the rate so paid.*

Where the owner has become liable to the payment of the poor rates, the rates due from him, together with the costs and charges of levying and recovering the same, may be levied on the goods of the owner, and be recovered from him in the same way as poor rates may be recovered from the occupier.†

Notwithstanding the owner of any hereditament has become liable for payment of the poor rates assessed thereon, the goods and chattels of the occupier are liable to be distrained and sold for payment of such rates as may accrue during his occupation of the premises, at any time whilst such rates remain unpaid by the owner, subject to the following provisions :—

1. That no such distress shall be levied unless the rate has been demanded, in writing, by the overseers from the occupier, and the occupier has failed to pay the same within fourteen days after the service of such demand.

2. That no greater sum shall be raised by such distress than shall, at the time of making the same, be actually due from the occupier for rent of the premises on which the distress is made.

* Sec. 8.   † Sec. 11.

3. That any such occupier shall be entitled to
   deduct the amount of rates for which such
   distraint is made, and the expense of distraint,
   from the rent due, or accruing due, to the
   owner; and every such payment shall be a
   valid discharge of the rent to the extent of
   the rate and expenses paid.*

The remaining clauses of the act are chiefly important for their bearing on the parliamentary franchise
of the occupiers of houses whose landlords compound
for the rates. Regarded in that light, they fall without
the scope of the present work; but it is desirable to
remind persons who may fill the office of overseer, of
the responsibility they incur under clause 19, which
provides that "overseers, in making out the poor
rate, shall, in every case, enter in the occupiers'
column of the rate-book the name of the occupier
of every rateable hereditament; and if any overseer negligently or wilfully, and without reasonable cause, omits the name of the occupier of any
rateable hereditament from the rate, or negligently or
wilfully misstates any name therein, such overseer
shall, for every such omission or misstatement, be
liable, on summary conviction, to a penalty not
exceeding £2.

* Sec. 12.

CHAPTER XXI.

OF PAROCHIAL ASSESSMENT.

PAROCHIAL assessment is now regulated by the Acts of 1862 and 1864; * the leading provisions of which will be found stated—necessarily with some brevity—in the following pages.

The board of guardians of every union, at their first meeting after the annual election, are to appoint from among themselves any number, not less than six, nor more than twelve, to be a committee, consisting partly of *ex-officio* and partly of elected guardians (called the assessment committee of the union) for the investigation and supervision of the valuations to be made within such union.

Where any union has the same bounds as a municipal borough, the town council may, if they think fit, appoint from themselves a certain number not exceeding the number appointed by the board of guardians, to form part of the assessment committee for such union.

The committee may from time to time require the overseers, assistant overseers, constables, assessors, collectors, and any other persons having the custody of any books of assessment of any taxes or rates, parliamentary or parochial, or of the valuations of any parish, or having the collection or management of any

* 25 & 26 Vict. c. 103 ; and 27 & 28 Vict. c. 39.

such taxes or rates, to make returns in writing, to the committee, of all such particulars as the latter may direct, in relation to such taxes, rates, or valuations, or any property included therein, so far as relates to the union for which they act : or to produce such books to the committee, or to attend them and submit to a personal examination.

Subject to any order which may be made by the committee, the overseers of each parish in the union, must, within three calendar months after the appointment of such committee, make a list of all the rateable hereditaments in such parish, with the annual value thereof.*

The committee may from time to time direct any existing valuation of a parish to be revised, or a new valuation to be made by the overseers ; or may, with the consent of the board of guardians, appoint some person to perform either of the duties just mentioned.

And by the Poor Law Amendment Act, 1868 (31 & 32 Vict. c. 122, s. 38), the guardians may, upon the application of the assessment committee, appoint some competent person to assist the committee in the valuation of the rateable hereditaments of the parish for such a period as they shall see fit, at a salary or other settled remuneration to be paid out of the common fund.

The valuation list, when made out, is to be open to the inspection of ratepayers.

---

* The gross estimated rental is to be the rent at which the hereditament might reasonably be expected to let from year to year, free of all usual tenant's rates and taxes and tithe commutation rent-charge, if any.

Any overseer who thinks that his parish, or any person who feels himself aggrieved by any valuation list, on the ground of unfairness or incorrectness, may give the committee a notice in writing of his objection. The committee are then to hold such meetings as they may think necessary for hearing objections to the valuation list, and whether any objection be or be not made to any such list, they may direct further valuation, may correct the valuation list, and, when correct, may approve the same.

If on appeal to the sessions against any rate, it be amended,* the valuation list must be altered accordingly.

When property not included in the valuation list in force in any parish becomes rateable, or any rateable property included in such list has been increased, or reduced in value since the valuation, the overseers may make a supplemental valuation list, showing the annual rateable value of such property ; and the committee may, from time to time, direct a new valuation, and new or supplemental valuation lists to be prepared.

In every parish where a valuation list under this act has been approved and delivered to the overseers, no rate for the relief of the poor, or other rate which by law is required to be based upon the poor rate, will be of any force, unless the hereditaments included in such rate are rated according to the annual rateable value thereof appearing in the valuation list in force in such parish.†

* See Chapter XIX.
† The provisions of the section here abstracted do not apply

If the overseer or overseers of any parish in a union "shall have reason to think that such parish is aggrieved by the valuation list of any parish within such union, whether it be on the ground that the rateable hereditaments comprised in the valuation list of such parish are valued at sums beyond the annual rateable value thereof, or on the ground that the rate able hereditaments comprised in the valuation list of some other parish in such union are valued at sums less than the annual rateable value thereof," such overseer or overseers may, with the consent of a vestry specially summoned to consider the subject, appeal to the quarter sessions against such valuation list. But notice of such appeal must be given to the assessment committee of the union, who may, with the consent of the guardians, appear as respondents. The costs which the committee may thus incur (if not recovered from the appellants) as well as any costs the committee may be ordered to pay to the appellants, are to be paid by the guardians and charged to the common fund of the union, unless the court before whom the appeal is heard direct that such costs, or any part thereof, shall be charged to the parish, the rate of which is appealed against.

We have hitherto spoken of the kingdom generally. But we ought to add, that the valuation of property in London is still further regulated and governed by an act passed in 1869 (32 & 33 Vict. c. 67) the object

to any poor rate made by any vestry, trustees, guardians, commissioners, overseers, or other persons authorized by any local act to make the rate for the relief of the poor in any parish, or the assessment on which such rate is made.

of which was to secure uniformity of assessment throughout the metropolis. Into the details of this somewhat complicated measure we cannot enter, but we may say generally, that it seeks to accomplish its main object by concentrating the revision of the assessments made for each parish in a general assessment sessions, consisting of justices appointed by the magistrates of the counties of Middlesex, Surrey, and Kent, and by the mayor and aldermen of the city. To that body is entrusted the duty of hearing appeals from any part of the metropolis, and of considering and investigating complaints that the assessment of any parish or parishes is either higher or lower than it ought to be in reference to the general valuation of property throughout the district.

CHAPTER XXII.

OF THE POWERS OF THE LOCAL GOVERNMENT BOARD IN THE ADMINISTRATION OF THE POOR LAWS.

THE general administration of the poor laws is subject to the regulation and direction of the Local Government board, to whom all the power and duties formerly vested in the poor law board were transferred by an act passed in 1870. They are authorized to make rules, orders, and regulations for the management of the poor, for the government of workhouses, for the education of the children therein, for apprenticing the children of the poor, for the guidance and control of all guardians, vestries, and parish officers, so far as

relates to the management or relief of the poor and
the making or entering into contracts in all matters
relating to the same, and the keeping, examining,
auditing, and allowing of accounts, and generally for
carrying into effect the statute 4 & 5 Will. IV c. 76
(the new Poor Law as it is popularly called); and
they may alter, suspend, or rescind these rules, &c.,
at their discretion. So they may, by order under
their hands and seals, prescribe the duties of the
masters to whom poor children may be apprenticed,
and the terms and conditions to be inserted in the
indentures by which such children may be so bound as
apprentices, and every master who wilfully refuses or
neglects to perform any of such terms or conditions so
inserted in any such indenture is liable, upon conviction thereof before any two justices, to forfeit any
sum not exceeding £20. But the board cannot interfere in any individual case for the purpose of ordering
relief, nor can they make any rule, &c., which may
have the effect of compelling the inmates of workhouses to attend a mode of worship contrary to their
religious principles, or of causing children to be edu-
cated in such workhouses in any religious creed to
which their parents may object. The Queen in council
may at any time annul any orders of the board, but
so long, however, as they remain in force, if "any
person shall wilfully neglect or disobey any of the
rules, orders, or regulations of the said commissioners
or assistant commissioners, or be guilty of any contempt of the said commissioners sitting as a board,
such person shall, upon conviction before any two justices, forfeit and pay for the first offence any sum not

exceeding £5, for the second offence any sum not exceeding £20 nor less than £5, and in the event of any such person being convicted a third time, such third and every subsequent offence shall be deemed a misdemeanor, and such offender shall be liable to be indicted for the same offence, and shall, on conviction, pay such fine, not being less than £20, and suffer such imprisonment, with or without hard labour, as may be awarded against him by the court by or before which he shall be tried and convicted."

The board may, by their order, declare so many parishes as they think fit, united for the administration of the poor laws; and such parishes shall thereupon be deemed a UNION for such purpose, and the workhouse belonging thereto shall be for common use. The board may also now dissolve and re-arrange unions at their pleasure.

The power of the Local Government board in regard to the formation of unions is, indeed, subject to one qualification. By the 7 & 8 Vict. c. 101, s. 64, it is provided, that when the relief of the poor has been hitherto administered in any parish by guardians appointed under a local act, and not by overseers of the poor, if such parish, according to the last census, contain more than 20,000 persons, it shall not be lawful for the said commissioners, after the passing of that act, without the consent in writing of at least two-thirds of such guardians, to declare such parish to be united with any other parish for the administration of the laws for the relief of the poor. But then by the 30 & 31 Vict. c. 106, s. 2, if the guardians of any parish (except in the metropolis) at present governed

M

by a local act, apply * to the Local Government
board to repeal or alter such local act, the board may
issue a provisional order for the purpose, subject, of
course, like other provisional orders of the same kind,
to confirmation by an act of parliament, which the
board will itself take the necessary steps to carry
through parliament.

The board, with the consent in writing of the
guardians of an union, or of a majority of the ratepayers and overseers in a parish not having a workhouse, may order one to be built, and money borrowed
for that purpose may be charged upon the rates.   Or,
where there is already a workhouse, the commissioners
may order it to be enlarged or altered without such
consent, if the sum required for the purpose will not
exceed £50, or a tenth of the year's rate.

The board have power to institute inquiries, on oath,
into all matters connected with the administration of
an union ; and they may also require from all persons
in whom property is vested, in trust for the poor of
the parish, or who are in the receipt of the rents or
profits of such property, detailed particulars of the
same, and of the manner in which it is appropriated.

The board are assisted in their duties by "inspectors," to each of whom a district is allotted.   These
officers are entitled to visit and inspect every workhouse or place wherein any poor person in receipt of
relief shall be lodged, and to attend every board of
guardians, and every parochial and other local meeting
held for the relief of the poor, and to take part in the

* The application must be agreed to by a majority at two
successive meetings of the board.

proceedings, but not to vote at such board or meeting. And they have, also, the power to institute inquiries into the administration of the poor laws, and to compel the attendance of persons,* and the production of papers. They have the power to administer an oath.

CHAPTER XXIII.

THE BOARD OF GUARDIANS.

WHEN parishes or townships are united, by order or with the concurrence of the Local Government board, for the administration of the laws for the relief of the poor, a board of guardians of the poor for the union is constituted by the appointment of one or more guardians for each parish or township in the union—the number being determined by the Local Government board, who also fix their qualification, which consists in being rated to the poor within the union, at such a sum as the board may appoint, so that it does not exceed an annual rateable value of £40. But no assistant overseer in any parish, no paid officer engaged in the poor-law administration, no person who, having been such paid officer, shall have been dismissed from his office within five years previously, nor any person receiving any emolument from the poor rates in any parish or union, is capable of serving as a guardian in such parish or union.

* Provided always that no person shall be required, in obedience to the summons, to go or travel more than ten miles from his place of abode.

The board of guardians is a corporation.

The guardians in each parish of the union are elected *—1st, By the ratepayers who have been rated to the poor the whole of the year preceding, and have paid their poor rates for one whole year, and all due up to the time of voting, except those due within the six months immediately preceding; and 2ndly, By the owners of property within the parish who have, previously to the 1st February preceding the day of voting, given a statement in writing of their name and address, and the description of their property, to the overseers.† In every case in which a parish contains more than 20,000 persons, the local government board may, for the purpose of conducting the election of guardians, divide it into as many wards as they deem expedient (but so that no ward shall contain a greater number of rated houses than 400), and may determine the number of guardians to be elected for every such ward.

Each owner and each ratepayer owning or occupying property the annual value of which is under £50 has one vote; £50, and under £100, two votes; £100, and less than £150, three votes; £150, and less than £200, four votes; £200, and less than £250, five votes; and if it amount to or exceed £250, six votes;

* The ratepayers of any parish may re-elect those who have been guardians for the preceding year; or they may choose those who have already been elected as guardians for any other parish.

† Corporations and joint-stock and other companies may vote by one of their officers appointed by them for the purpose, notice thereof being previously given to the overseers, in the same manner as by owners of property.

*and where the owner is also the occupier, he may vote
as well in respect of his occupation as of his being such
owner.* But no person can give, in the whole of the
wards into which a parish may be divided, a greater
number of votes than he would have been entitled to
give if the parish had not been divided into wards;
nor in any one ward a greater number of votes than
he is entitled to in respect of property in that ward.
Any ratepayer or owner may, however, by notice in
writing signed by him, and delivered to the overseers
of the parish before the day appointed for the annual
nomination of candidates, elect in which ward or
wards he will vote for the ensuing year. Owners
may vote by proxy, if they do not reside in the
parish.

The votes are given by voting papers, which
are to be collected and returned as the Local Government board direct. The election of guardians takes
place on the 25th * day of March, or within forty days
after; and the guardians elected remain in office until
the 15th April in the year following. Before the 26th
of March, the overseers are to distinguish in the rate-
book the names of the ratepayers qualified to vote at
the election of guardians. Then, before the 15th
March, the clerk of the board of guardians is to prepare and sign a notice containing the following particulars :—

* Whenever any day appointed for the performance of **any**
act relating to or connected with the election of guardians
falls on Sunday or Good Friday, such act is to be performed on
the day following, and each subsequent proceeding shall be
postponed one day.

1. The number of guardians to be elected for each parish in the union.
2. The qualification of guardians.
3. The persons by whom, and the places where, the nomination papers in respect of each parish are to be received, and the last day on which they are to be sent.
4. The mode of voting in case of a contest, and the days on which the voting papers will be delivered and collected.
5. The time and place for the examination and casting up of the votes.

And the clerk is to cause such notice to be published on or before the 15th day of March, in the following manner :—

1. A printed copy of such notice shall be affixed on the principal external gate or door of every workhouse in the union, and shall, from time to time, be renewed, if necessary, until the 9th day of April.
2. Printed copies of such notice shall likewise be affixed on such places, in each of the parishes of the union, as are ordinarily made use of for fixing thereon notices of parochial business.

Any person entitled to vote in any parish, may nominate for the office of guardian thereof himself or any other person or persons (not exceeding the number of guardians to be elected for such parish), provided that the person or persons so nominated be legally qualified to be elected to that office.

The nomination is to be in writing, and to be sent in to the clerk of the board of guardians after the 14th and before the 26th of March. If no more candidates are nominated than the number of guardians required to be appointed, there will, of course, be no contest; but should this not be the case, and should there be a contest, it is to be conducted in the following manner (we give the articles of the order, in consequence of the interest which attaches to this subject, and the frequent disputes to which it gives rise) :—

Art. 10. But if the number of the duly qualified persons nominated for the office of guardians of any parish shall exceed the number of guardians to be elected therein, the clerk shall cause voting papers to be prepared and filled up, and shall insert therein the names of all the persons nominated, in the order in which the nomination papers were received; but it shall not be necessary to insert more than once the name of any person nominated.

Art. 11. The clerk shall, on the 5th day of April, cause one of such voting papers to be delivered, by the persons appointed for that purpose, to the address in such parish of each ratepayer, owner, and proxy qualified to vote therein.

Art. 12. If the clerk considers that any person nominated is not duly qualified to be a guardian, he shall state in the voting paper the fact that such person has been nominated, but that he considers such person not to be duly qualified.

Art. 13. If any person put in nomination for the office of guardian in any parish shall tender to the officer conducting the election his refusal in writing to serve such office, and if in consequence of such refusal the number of persons nominated for the office of guardian for such parish shall be the same as or less than the number of guardians to be elected for such parish, all, or so many of the remaining candidates as shall be duly qualified, shall be deemed to be the elected guardians for such parish for the ensuing year, and shall be certified as such by the clerk under his hand as hereinafter provided in *Art*. 22.

Art. 14. Each voter shall write his initials in the voting paper delivered to him against the name or names of the person or persons (not exceeding the number of guardians to be elected in the parish) for whom he intends to vote, and shall sign such voting paper; and when any person votes as a proxy, he shall in like manner write his own initials and sign his own name, and state also in writing the name of the person for whom he is proxy.

Art. 15. Provided that if any voter cannot write, he shall affix his mark at the foot of the voting paper in the presence of a witness, who shall attest the affixing thereof, and shall write the name of the voter against such mark, as well as the initials of such voter against the name of every candidate for whom the voter intends to vote.

Art. 16. If the initials of the voter be written against the names of more persons than are to be elected guardians for the parish, or if the voter do not sign or affix his mark to the voting paper, or if his mark be not duly attested, or his name be not duly written by the witness, or if a proxy do not sign his own name and state in writing the name of the person for whom he is proxy, such voter shall be omitted in the calculation of votes.

Art. 17 The clerk shall cause the voting papers to be collected on the 7th day of April, by the persons appointed or employed for that purpose, in such manner as he shall direct.

Art. 18. No voting paper shall be received or admitted unless the same have been delivered at the address in each parish of the voter, and collected by the persons employed for that purpose, except as is provided in *Art.* 19.*

Art. 19. Provided that every person qualified to vote, who shall not on the 5th day of April have received a voting paper, shall, on application before the 8th day of April to the clerk at his office, be entitled to receive a voting paper, and to fill up the same in the presence of the clerk, and then and there to deliver the same to him.

Art. 20. Provided also that in case any voting paper duly delivered shall not have been collected through

* With regard to the election of the board of guardians, it is provided by the 14 & 15 Vict. c. 105, s. 3, that "if any person, pending or after the election of any guardian or guardians, shall wilfully, fraudulently, and with intent to affect the result of such election, commit any of the acts following :— that is to say, fabricate, in whole or in part, alter, deface, destroy, abstract, or purloin any nomination or voting paper used therein ; or personate any person entitled to vote at such election ; or falsely assume to act in the name or on behalf of any person so entitled to vote ; or interrupt the distribution or collection of the voting papers ; or distribute or collect the same under a false pretence of being lawfully authorized to do so :—every person so offending shall, for every such offence, be liable, upon conviction thereof before any two justices, to be imprisoned in the common gaol or house of correction for any period not exceeding three months, with or without hard labour."

the default of the clerk, or the persons appointed or employed for that purpose, the voter in person may deliver the same to the clerk before twelve o'clock at noon on the 8th day of April.

Art. 21. The clerk shall, on the 9th day of April, and on as many days immediately succeeding as may be necessary, attend at the board-room of the guardians of the union, and ascertain the validity of the votes by an examination of the rate-books, and the registers of owners and proxies, and such other documents as he may think necessary, and by examining such persons as he may see fit ; and he shall cast up such of the votes as he shall find to be valid, and to have been duly given, collected, or received, and ascertain the number of such votes for each candidate.

Art. 22. The candidates, to the number of guardians to be elected for the parish, who, being duly qualified, shall have obtained the greatest number of votes, shall be deemed to be the elected guardians of the parish, and shall be certified as such by the clerk under his hand.

Art. 23. The clerk, when he shall have ascertained that any candidate is duly elected as a guardian, shall notify the fact of his having been so elected by delivering, or sending, or causing to be delivered or sent to him, a notice in the form in the schedule to these ules annexed.

Art. 24. The clerk shall make a list containing the names of the candidates, together with (in case of a contest) the number of votes given for each, and the names of the elected guardians, in the form in the schedule to these rules annexed, and shall sign and certify the same, and shall deliver such list, together with all the nomination and voting papers which he shall have received, to the guardians of the union at their next meeting, who shall preserve the same for a period of not less than two years.

Art. 25. The clerk shall cause copies of such list to be printed, and shall deliver, or send, or cause to be delivered or sent, one or more of such copies to the overseers of each parish.

Art. 26. The overseers shall affix, or cause to be affixed, copies of such list at the usual places for affixing in each parish notices of parochial business.

Art. 27 In case of the decease, necessary absence, refusal, or disqualification to act during the proceedings of the election, of the clerk or any other person appointed or employed to act, in respect of such election, the delivery of the nominations, voting papers, or other documents to the successor of the clerk or person so dying, absenting himself, refusing, or disqualified to act, shall, notwithstanding the terms of any notice issued, be as valid and effectual as if they had been delivered to such clerk or person.*

The validity of disputed elections to the office of guardian may be inquired into by the Local Government board, if they think fit.

Besides the elected guardians, all the justices of the peace residing in the union, and acting for the county,

* The articles of the general order of the 24th July, 1847, which we have given above, and which in substance govern the mode of election, are still in force, but many modifications of the minor details of the election have been made by subsequent orders signed in 1867 and 1868.

riding, or division in which the same is situated, are *ex officio* members of the board.

The duties of the board of guardians may be stated generally—to govern the workhouse and administer poor-law relief according to the orders of the local government board.* By those orders they are directed to hold meetings every week or fortnight. They are to appoint at their first meeting a chairman and vice-chairman. Three are constituted a quorum. Extra-ordinary meetings may be called by a requisition of two guardians addressed to the clerk. And in case of emergency requiring that a meeting of the guardians shall take place immediately, they, or any three of them, may meet at the ordinary place of meeting, and take such case into consideration, and make an order thereon. Questions coming before them are to be decided by a majority of those present and voting; and no resolution, once passed, shall be rescinded or altered by them, unless some guardian shall have given to the board seven days' notice of a motion to alter or rescind such resolution, which notice shall be forthwith entered on the minutes by the clerk.

At every ordinary meeting of the board of guardians, the business is, as far as may be, to be conducted in the following order:—

1. The minutes of the last ordinary meeting, and of any other meeting which may have been held since such ordinary meeting, shall be read to the guardians, and in order that such minutes may be recognized as a record of the acts of the guardians at their last

* Their duties in regard to the removal of nuisances are stated in a previous chapter.

meeting, they shall be signed by the chairman presiding at the meeting at which such minutes are read, and an entry of the same having been so read shall be made in the minutes of the day when read.

2. The guardians shall dispose of such business as may arise out of the minutes so read, and shall give the necessary directions thereon.

3. They shall proceed to give the necessary directions respecting all applications for relief made since the last ordinary meeting, and also respecting the amount and nature of relief to be given and continued to the paupers then in the receipt of relief until the next ordinary meeting, or for such other time as such relief may be deemed to be necessary.

4. They shall hear and consider any application for relief which may be then made, and determine thereon.

5. They shall read the report of the state of the workhouse or workhouses, examine all books and accounts relative to the relief of the paupers of the union, and give all needful directions concerning the management and discipline of the said workhouse or workhouses, and the providing of furniture, stores, and other articles.

6. They shall examine the treasurer's account, and shall, when necessary, make orders on the overseers or other proper authorities of the several parishes in the union for providing such sums as may be lawfully required by the guardians on account of the respective parishes.

The consolidated order of July, 1847, regulates in a very stringent manner the mode in which the guardians are to purchase articles or enter into contracts, and as the observance of these provisions is of the last importance (for the Local Government Board may avoid all contracts made in violation of them), while at the same time they furnish the best protection against any corruption in parochial transactions, we give them entire :—

Art. 44. All contracts to be entered into on behalf of the union relating to the maintenance, clothing, lodging, employment, or relief of the poor, or for any other purpose relating to or connected with the general management of the poor, shall be made and entered into by the guardians.*

Art. 45. The guardians shall require tenders to be made in some sealed paper for the supply of all provisions, fuel, clothing, furniture, or other goods or materials, the consumption of which may be estimated one month with another to exceed £10 per month, and of all provisions, fuel, clothing, furniture, or other goods or materials, the cost of which may be reasonably estimated to exceed £50 in a single sum, and shall purchase the same upon contracts to be entered into after the receipt of such tenders.

Art. 46. Any work or repairs to be executed in the workhouse or the premises connected with the workhouse, or any fixture to be put up therein which may respectively be reasonably estimated to exceed the cost of £50 in one sum, shall be contracted for by the guardians on sealed tenders in the manner prescribed in articles 45 and 47.

Art. 47. Notice of the nature and conditions of the

* They must be sealed with the corporate seal of the board.

contract to be entered into, of the estimated amount of the articles required, of the last day on which tenders will be received, and the day on which the tenders will be opened, shall be given in some newspaper circulating in the union not less than ten days previous to the last day on which such tenders are to be received; and no tender shall be opened by the clerk or any guardian or other person prior to the day specified in such notice, or otherwise than at a meeting of the said guardians.

Art. 48. When any tender is accepted, the party making the tender shall, in pursuance of these regulations, enter into a contract in writing with the guardians, containing the terms, conditions, and stipulations mutually agreed upon ; and whenever the guardians deem it advisable, the party contracting shall find one or more surety or sureties who shall enter into a bond conditioned for the due performance of the contract, or shall otherwise secure the same.

Art. 49. Provided always, that, if from the peculiar nature of any provisions, fuel, clothing, furniture, goods, materials, or fixtures to be supplied, or of any work or repairs to be executed, it shall appear to the guardians desirable that a specific person or persons be employed to supply or execute the same without requiring sealed tenders as hereinbefore directed, it shall be lawful for such guardians, with the consent of the commissioners first obtained, to enter into a contract with the said person or persons, and to require such surety and sureties as are specified in *Art.* 48.

Art. 50. Every contract to be hereafter made by

any guardians shall contain a stipulation requiring the
contractor to send in his bill on account of the sum
due to him for goods or work on or before some day
to be named in the contract.

Art. 51. The guardians shall fix some day or days,
not being more than twenty-one days after the end of
each quarter, for the attendance of contractors and
tradesmen, or their authorized agents, and the clerk
shall notify such day to every contractor or tradesman
to whom money may be due, or to his agent, or he
shall, under the direction of guardians, cause the
same to be advertised in some newspaper.

It is necessary, moreover, that all guardians and
union officers should bear carefully in mind that, under
the 4 & 5 Wm. 4, c. 76, ss. 51 and 57, any guardian or person concerned in the administration of the
poor laws, who is concerned in contracts for, or who
supplies for his own profit, goods furnished for the
relief of the poor, is subjected to a penalty. While
by the 89th section of the same statute, it is provided,
that all payments made by guardians, and charged
upon the poor rates contrary to the provisions of the
act, or at variance with any rule, &c., of the commissioners, are illegal, and are to be disallowed.

Then as to payments it is ordered that,—

The guardians shall pay every sum greater than £5
by an order, which shall be drawn upon the treasurer
of the union, and shall be signed by the presiding
chairman and two other guardians at a meeting, and
shall be countersigned by the clerk. The guardians
shall examine at their board, or cause to be examined
by some committee or guardian authorized by them

for the purpose, every bill exceeding in amount £1 (except the salaries of officers) brought against the union; and when any such bill has been allowed by the board, or by such committee or guardian, a note of the allowance thereof shall be made on the face of the bill before the amount is paid.

By a statute passed in the year 1859 (22 & 23 Vict. c. 49, s. 1), it is enacted that, "with respect to any debt, claim, or demand which may, after the passing of this act, be lawfully incurred or become due from the guardians of any union or parish, or the board of management of any school or asylum district, such debt, claim, or demand shall be paid within the half-year in which the same shall have been incurred or become due, or within three months after the expiration of such half-year, but not afterwards—the commencement of such half-year to be reckoned from the time when the last half-year's account shall or ought to have closed, according to the order of the poor-law commissioners or poor-law board: provided that the poor-law board by their order may, if they see fit, extend the time within which such payment shall be made for a period not exceeding twelve months after the date of such debt, claim, or demand." And by section 2, "with respect to any debt, claim, or demand, which may have been lawfully incurred by any such guardians or board of management, or on their account, before the passing of this act, they may, if they think proper, pay, within twelve months after the passing of this act, out of the funds in their possession, any such debt, claim, or demand which may have been so incurred or have become due within two

N

years before the date of this act, and may, within the said period of twelve months, make provision for the payment of any debt, claim, or demand lawfully incurred as aforesaid which shall have become due from them at some time beyond two years, but not beyond six years, from such date, in full at once or by equal annual instalments not exceeding five, if the poor-law board (after open and public investigation, during which counsel and solicitors may appear, and witnesses may be examined on both sides, when the same shall be required by any ratepayer of the union, parish, or district), shall be satisfied that no fraud, collusion, or neglect of the general rules of the poor-law board respecting the contraction or discharge of such debt, claim, or demand have been committed by the party to whom such claim or demand is alleged to be due, and that such party has not been accessory to any fraud on such guardians or board of management, and shall give their assent in manner aforesaid to such payment; and such guardians or board respectively shall charge every such payment to the account to which the same would have been charged if the payment had been made in due time; and the president or secretary of the poor-law board shall, within one calendar month after the expiration of such period of twelve months as aforesaid, if parliament be then sitting, or if not, within one calendar month after the next · meeting thereof, lay or cause to be. laid before both houses of parliament a return of all such payments as shall have been made or authorized under the power herein lastly contained."

It is lawful for the guardians, or, where there are

no guardians, for the overseers, to bury the body of
any poor person who may be within their parish or
union respectively, and to charge the expense thereof
to any parish under their control to which such person
may have been chargeable, or in which he may have
died, or in which the body may be. And the interment is to take place in consecrated ground, unless the
deceased person or the husband or wife or next of kin
of such person have otherwise desired. In the case of
a destitute wayfarer or wanderer or foundling dying
in a union, the costs of burial are to be charged to
the common fund of the union. And in connection
with this part of our subject, it may be as well to mention that, under the 13 & 14 Vict. c. 101, s. 2, the
guardians are empowered to contribute out of the
common fund to the enlargement of any churchyard
or consecrated burial-ground in the union, or to the
obtaining of such consecrated burial-ground; while,
by the 18 & 19 Vict. c. 77, they may enter into agreements with the proprietors of any cemetery established
under the authority of parliament, or with any burial-
board duly constituted under the statutes in that
behalf, for the burial of the dead bodies of any poor
persons which such guardians or overseers may undertake to bury, or towards the burial whereof they may
render assistance.

The guardians are authorized, by the 7 & 8 Vict. c.
101, s. 59, to prosecute for various offences against
the poor laws, and to charge the costs thereof either
to the common fund of the union or to any parish or
parishes thereof. They are required, by the Vaccination Acts of 1867 and 1871, to provide for the

N 2

gratuitous vaccination, by competent medical men, of all persons resident in the union. And, by the 14 & 15 Vict. c. 105, s. 4, they are empowered, with the consent of the Local Government board, to pay an annual subscription out of the union funds towards the support of a public hospital or infirmary.

We have hitherto spoken of boards of guardians of unions, but the Local Government board may direct that a board of guardians shall be elected for a single parish. In that case the parish will be divided into wards for the election of guardians. In other respects the law, as above stated, both with respect to election, qualification, voting, &c., and also as to proceedings, powers, &c., is exactly the same as in the case where a union is formed.

CHAPTER XXIV.

OF METROPOLITAN DISTRICT ASYLUM BOARDS, AND THE METROPOLIS COMMON POOR FUND.

IT had long been admitted that it was desirable to deal with the relief of the poor in the metropolis in a more comprehensive way, and with reference to larger areas, than was possible so long as each union or parish was a separate district, complete in itself, and independent of any other. It had also become expedient to equalize in some degree the burthen of pauperism, which was found to press with undue severity on some, and with undue lightness on other parishes or unions. Nothing, however, was done to attain either of these objects until 1867, when the Metropolitan Poor Act (30 Vict. c. 6) was passed. Of this measure (which was amended by 32 & 33 Vict. c. 63) it is impossible for us to offer more than a brief sketch. But on the other hand, some notice of the principal provisions of a measure which affects in so vital a manner the administration of the poor law in the capital of the country, seems indispensable to a work like the present.

Under these acts, the Poor Law board were, and the Local Government board are, authorized to divide the metropolis into districts, in each of which an asylum or asylums are to be provided for the reception and relief of the sick, insane, infirm, or other class or classes of the poor chargeable on the unions or parishes of the metropolis.

The asylum or asylums of each district are placed under a board of managers, two-thirds, at least, of whom are elected by the guardians of the several unions or parishes forming the district, either from amongst themselves, or from ratepayers qualified to be guardians, while the remaining third may be nominated by the Local Government board from among justices of the peace for any county or place, resident in the district, or from among ratepayers resident in the district, and assessed to the poor rate therein on an annual rateable value of not less than £40.

The Local Government board may from time to time direct the managers to purchase, lease, or build, and (in either case) to fit up a building for the asylum, of such nature and size, and in such a manner, as the board think fit. For the purpose of defraying the expense the managers may borrow money on the secu-

rity of the rates.* Or an existing workhouse may, with
such alterations as the local government board think
fit, be converted into a district asylum, in which case
a rent will be payable for its use to the guardians of
the union to which it belongs.

The expense incurred by the managers in purchasing,
leasing, building, repairing, and fitting up asylums, or
any sum payable as rent in respect of them, together
with " the expenses incurred by the managers in or about
the providing of fixtures, furniture, conveniences,
medicines, medical and surgical appliances, and other
necessaries required for keeping the asylum in proper
order for daily use, and the salaries and maintenance
of the officers thereof, *are to be defrayed by contributions
from the unions and parishes forming the district.*" †
But on the other hand, " the expenses incurred by the
managers in and about the food, clothing, maintenance,
care, treatment, and relief, or for the burials, of inmates
of the asylum, are *to be separately charged to the
respective unions or parishes from which the inmates of
the asylum are sent.*"

Provision is next made for the establishment of
dispensaries in such unions or parishes as the Local
Government board may direct; for the erection, &c.,
of district schools for the pauper children of unions or
parishes united together; for assigning particular workhouses in the metropolis to different classes of inmates;
and for some other matters of less importance.

* As to the conditions and limitations under which this
may be done, see 30 Vict. c. 6, s. 17.

† These contributions will, of course, be in proportion to
the rateable value of the property in each union or parish.

The act then provides for the creation of a " Metropolitan Common Poor Fund," raised by contributions from the several unions and parishes in London, in proportion to the annual rateable value of the property comprised therein.   Out of this common fund are repaid all the expenses incurred by the several unions and parishes for the following purposes :—

" 1. For the maintenance of lunatics in asylums, registered hospitals and benevolent houses, and insane poor in asylums, under this act,* except such as are chargeable on the county rate.

" 2. For the maintenance of patients in any asylum specially provided under this act for patients suffering from fever or small-pox.

" 3. For all medicines and medical and surgical appliances supplied to the poor in receipt of relief by guardians under this act or any of the poorlaw acts.

" 4. For the salaries of all the officers employed by the guardians in and about the relief of the poor, by the managers of district schools, under ' The Poor Law Amended Act, 1844,' and by the managers of asylums under this act, and also the salaries of the dispensers and other persons employed in dispensaries under the act, provided the appointment of the officers have been sanctioned by the Poor-law (Local Government) Board.

" 5. For compensation to any medical officer of a workhouse affected by the determination or variation

* By "this act," here and throughout the following paragraphs, must be understood the Metropolitan Poor Act, 1867.

by the Poor-law (Local Government) **Board of**
a contract respecting medical relief in the workhouse, or for compensation to any officer of a
union or parish who may be deprived of his
office by reason of the operation of this act.

" 6 For fees for registration of births and deaths.

" 7. For fees for, and other expenses of, vaccination.

" 8. For maintenance of pauper children in district,
separate, certificated, and licensed schools.

" 9. For the relief of destitute persons, and provision of places of reception for them, under
the Metropolitan Houseless Poor Acts of 1864
and 1865."

By throwing these charges on a common fund, raised
by contributions in proportion to rateable value, the
burthen of the pauperism of the metropolis is to a
large extent equalized.

CHAPTER XXV.

OF THE POWERS OF JUSTICES OF THE PEACE IN THE ADMINISTRATION OF THE POOR LAWS.

THE authority of justices of the peace in giving relief
in unions or in parishes under the government of a
select vestry, is limited by the New Poor Law Act to
the following cases :—

1. In cases of " sudden and urgent necessity," overseers shall give temporary relief as each case shall
require in articles of absolute necessity, but not in
money; and if any overseer shall refuse or neglect to give
such necessary relief, in any such case of necessity, to

poor persons not settled nor usually residing in the parish to which' such overseer belongs, any justice of the peace, by writing under his hand and seal, may order the said overseer to give such temporary relief, in articles of absolute necessity, as the case shall require, but not in money; and in case such overseer shall disobey such order, he shall, on conviction before two justices, forfeit a sum not exceeding £5.

2. Any justice of the peace may give a similar order for medical relief only, to any parishioner as well as to any out-parishioner, when any case of sudden and dangerous illness may require it, and any overseer shall be liable to the same penalties as aforesaid, for disobeying such order.

3. In any union which may be formed under the said statute, any two justices usually acting for the district in which the union may be situated, may, at their just and proper discretion, direct, by order under their hands and seals, that relief shall be given to any adult person, who shall, from old age or infirmity of body, be wholly unable to work, without requiring that such person shall reside in any workhouse—such person being entitled to relief in such union, and desiring to receive the same out of a workhouse; but one of such justices shall certify in such order, of his own knowledge, that such person is wholly unable to work as aforesaid.

In parishes not under a board of guardians or a select vestry, the justices may order the overseers to grant relief, subject to the rules and orders of the poor-law commissioners upon the subject.

Every justice of the peace residing in any parish of a union, or any extra-parochial place adjoining it, and acting for the county, riding, or division in which the same is situated, is an *ex-officio* guardian for the union. This is also the case when a single parish is placed under a board of guardians.

The justices of the peace have very extensive powers in the visitation of workhouses, for by the 35 Geo. 3, c. 49, s. 1, it is enacted, that "any justice of the peace, or any physician, surgeon, or apothecary, authorized for the purpose by warrant under the hand and seal of any such justice, or the officiating clergyman of the parish or place, duly authorized as aforesaid, may, at all times in the day-time, visit any parish workhouse or house kept or provided for the maintenance of the poor of any parish or place within the county, riding, liberty, or division wherein such justice shall be resident, and shall have jurisdiction, and examine into the state and condition of the poor people therein, and the food, clothing, and bedding of such poor people, and the state and condition of such house, and if, upon such visitation, the said justice so authorized shall find any cause or occasion for complaint, then such justice or person authorized may, if he think fit, certify the state and condition of such workhouse or poorhouse, and the state of the poor therein, and of their food, clothing, and bedding, to the next quarter sessions of the peace, to be held for such county, riding, liberty, or division, wherein such workhouse or poorhouse shall be situate; and such justice of the peace, or other person so authorized as aforesaid, shall cause the overseers of the poor,

or master or governor of the said workhouse or poorhouse of such parish or place, to be summoned to
appear at the same sessions, to answer such complaint;
and the justices at quarter sessions, on hearing the
parties on such complaint, shall make such orders and
regulations for removing the cause of such complaint,
as to them shall seem meet, and the parties shall abide
by and perform the same."

But as the delay which would take place under this
course of procedure might be very injurious to the
poor people, it is further provided by the same statute,
that if upon such visitation such justice or authorized
person "find any of the poor in a parish workhouse or
poorhouse afflicted with any contagious or infectious
disease, or in want of medical or other assistance, or
of sufficient or proper food, or requiring separation or
removal from the other poor in the said house," then
such justices shall apply to one or more other justices
of the same county, or such other authorized person
shall apply to two justices of the county, and certify
to him or them the state and condition of the poor in
such house, and thereupon the said justices shall "make
such order for the immediate procuring medical or
other assistance, or sufficient and proper food, or for
the separation or removal of such poor as shall be
afflicted with any contagious or infectious disease," in
such manner as they, under their hands and seals, shall
think proper to direct, until the next quarter sessions
of the peace for the county, &c.; at which quarter
sessions the said two justices are to certify the same,
under their hands and seals, to the justices there assembled, who may make such order for the further

relief of the poor in the said house as to them shall seem meet and proper."*

And by the Poor Law Amendment Act, which does not affect the power given by the above statute, it is further enacted, "that when any rules, orders, or regulations, or any bye-laws, shall be made or directed by the poor-law commissioners to be observed or enforced in any workhouse, any justice of the peace acting in and for the county, place, or jurisdiction in which such workhouse may be situate, may visit, inspect, and examine such workhouse at such times as he shall think proper, for the purpose of ascertaining whether such rules, orders, regulations, or bye-laws are, or have been, duly observed and obeyed in such workhouse, as well as for the purposes mentioned in the above statute ; and if in the opinion of such justice such rules, &c., or any of them, have not been duly observed and obeyed in such workhouse, such justice may summon the party offending to appear before any two justices of the peace, to answer any complaint touching the non-observance of such rules, and upon conviction such party for the first offence shall forfeit a sum not exceeding £5 ; for a second offence, a sum not exceeding £20, nor less than £5 ; and a third or subsequent offence shall be deemed a misdemeanor, and the party being convicted thereof on indictment, shall pay such fine, not less than £20, and suffer such imprisonment, with or without hard labour, as the court may direct."

* This act, however, does not extend to any poorhouse or workhouse in any district or districts incorporated or regulated by special act of parliament.

The justices have also authority:—1. As to removals. 2. In appointing overseers. 3. In allowing or disallowing overseers' accounts. 4. In allowing poor rates. Their powers under these heads will be found detailed in the chapters in which these subjects are treated of.

CHAPTER XXVI.

OF THE OVERSEERS.

OVERSEERS are appointed in every parish, under the celebrated statute, 43 Eliz. c. 2, which is generally considered as the foundation of the modern poor law. It is provided by this act, that the churchwardens of every parish shall be overseers of the poor, and it was formerly necessary that besides these there should be appointed as overseers, in each parish, two, three, or four, but not more of the inhabitants; such last-mentioned overseers to be substantial householders, and to be nominated yearly by two justices dwelling near the parish.* Under a recent statute, however,† if it appear that two overseers cannot be conveniently appointed from the inhabitant householders in any

---

* Peers and members of parliament, justices of the peace, aldermen of London, clergymen, dissenting ministers, practising barristers and attorneys, members of the College of Physicians, members of the College of Surgeons, apothecaries, officers of the courts of law, officers of the army and navy, even on half-pay, and officers of the customs and excise, are exempt from serving the office. Persons who, at the time of the proposed appointment, hold the office of Government overseer, are disqualified to be overseers.

† 29 & 30 Vict. c. 113, s 10.

parish, the justices may appoint one overseer only; while in any parish the same person may now be both an overseer and a churchwarden. The appointment must be in writing under the hand and seal of two justices, who must execute it in the presence of each other. And persons aggrieved by such appointment, whether the persons appointed, or the parishioners at large, may appeal to the next quarter sessions.*

If a person who has been appointed an overseer refuse, without sufficient cause, to fulfil the duties of the office, he may be indicted.

It was at one time necessary that an overseer should be a householder in the parish for which he was appointed. But now justices of the peace, in their respective special sessions for the appointment of over-

---

* In appointing overseers, the justices of the peace are not bound to pay any attention to the nomination or recommendation of the vestry of the parish. The appointment, as we have already mentioned, must be in writing, and under the hand and seal of two justices, executed in the presence of each other. It should appoint the parties "overseers" *eo nomine*, and state them to be substantial householders in the parish, or as the case may be; and it must state that the appointment is for a parish, township, &c., and show that it is within the magistrates' jurisdiction. It should express the time for which the appointment is made, as "for one year next ensuing," or "the present year." If made on a Sunday, it will be bad, unless under peculiar circumstances, and done *bonâ fide*. If two different appointments are made on the same day, the last is void; for when the appointment is once legally made, the magistrates' jurisdiction ceases. If the quarter sessions confirm the appointment on appeal, it may nevertheless be removed by *certiorari* into the Court of Queen's Bench, and may then be quashed for any defects appearing on its face, as shown by affidavit.

seers of the poor, upon the nomination and at the request of the inhabitants of any parish, in vestry assembled, may appoint any person who shall be assessed to the relief of the poor thereof, and shall be a householder resident within two miles from the church or chapel of such parish, or (when there shall be no church or chapel) shall be resident within one mile from the boundary of such parish, to be an overseer of the poor thereof; although such person so to be appointed shall not be a householder within the parish of which he shall be appointed overseer. Provided, however, that no person shall be appointed to, or compellable to serve, the office of overseer of the poor of any parish or place in which he shall not be a householder, unless he shall have consented to such appointment. Nor is that all. The justices are not in all cases bound even to appoint a ratepayer of the parish. If it appear to them that there is no inhabitant householder liable to be appointed, they may * appoint some inhabitant householder of an adjoining parish *willing* to serve, either with or without a salary.

It will be observed, that overseers were in the first instance appointed for parishes only ; but a subsequent statute, passed in the reign of Charles II., enabled the justices, where parishes were large and populous, to appoint overseers for each township or village, who should have as to that township or village the same powers as other overseers in relation to parishes. And where such separate appointments have been made before the 9th of August, 1844, they may still be made ; but, by the 7 & 8 Vict. c. 101, s. 22, it shall

* 29 & 30 Vict. c. 113, s. 10.

not be lawful after that day to appoint separate overseers for any township, or village, or other place for which, before the passing of that act, separate overseers had not been lawfully appointed.

Overseers of parishes situated in counties are appointed by special sessions of the justices for the division in which they are situated. And when the parish is in a municipal borough, the appointment is made by the justices of the peace having jurisdiction therein, whether these happen to be justices of the county or of the borough. They are directed* to be appointed annually on the 25th of March, or within fourteen days after it; but appointments made at another time are not void. If the magistrates fail to make the appointment, the Court of Queen's Bench will compel them by mandamus to do so. On the other hand, if either the person nominated or the parishioners feel themselves aggrieved by any appointment, they may appeal against it to the general quarter sessions.

The principal duty of the overseers is, in conjunction with the churchwardens, to levy a poor rate for the purpose of providing such sums as may be necessary to meet the expense of relieving the poor, the costs of collecting the same, and all other expenses which are by various acts of parliament charged upon the poor rate. Out of the rate so levied they are to pay over from time to time all such sums as, by any order of the guardians addressed to them in writing according to the form set forth by the order of the poor-law commissioners bearing date the 24th of July,

* By 54 Geo. 3, c. 91.

1847, shall be directed to be provided from the poor rates of the parish, and to pay over such sums to such person or persons, at such times or places, as by the same order shall be directed, and to take the receipt of such person or persons, and to produce such order and such receipt as their vouchers for such payments before the auditors in passing their quarterly accounts. And the same order directs the overseers to submit, within forty days after each of the following days, namely, Lady-day, Midsummer-day Michaelmas-day, and Christmas-day, to the auditors of the union or district, an account and balance-sheet exhibiting the amount collected by them and the amount disbursed by them during the quarter, together with the proper vouchers for the same. It also directs that the overseers shall enter in some book, to be from time to time provided for the purpose, the names and addresses of the owners and proxies who shall send statements of their claims to vote and the assessment of the poor rate on the property for which they respectively claim to vote. And by another order, dated March 17, 1847, they must keep a rate book; a book of receipts and payments; prepare for the auditor a balance-sheet of receipts and payments every half-year; and, whenever required by the auditor for the time being, or the poor-law commissioners, make a return of the property belonging to the parish. Under various statutes the overseers are also required, within fourteen days after the appointment of their successors, to account to them for the rates received and sums paid during their period of office, and to hand over to them any balance remaining in their hands. Their accounts must also be verified by

Q

oath or affirmation before two justices of the peace,
who may entertain objections to them, allow them,
or if unsatisfactory, disallow the whole, or any items
which involve an expenditure contrary to law. From
the decision of the justices an appeal lies to the
quarter sessions. So far as these statutes constitute a
check upon the expenditure of the overseers, they have
become practically inoperative since the passing of the
7 & 8 Vict. c. 101, under which district auditors
are appointed, but they are still in force, and outgoing overseers must therefore be careful both to
account to their successors within the time specified,
and also to verify their accounts before two justices.
The allowance of the accounts by the latter now follows, in general, as a matter of course.

They are to perform such duties, in connection with
the election of guardians for the union, as may be imposed upon them by any regulations of the Local
Government Board in force at the time.

The overseers in parishes under a board of guardians
or a select vestry are not to give poor-law relief other
than that ordered by the guardians or vestry, except in
case of absolute necessity, and then it is to be given in
articles of necessity, and not in money. But if they
neglect to give such temporary relief, when ordered by
a justice of the peace, they may be fined £5. And a
similar penalty is imposed upon their neglect to afford
medical relief, when ordered by a justice, in case
of urgency. The duties of overseers and churchwardens of parishes in unions in regard to relief are
thus further defined by the order of the Poor-law Board
of the 22nd of April, 1842 :—

Art. 1. If any overseer of the poor of any parish shall, in any case of sudden and urgent necessity, have given temporary relief in articles of necessity, or, in any case of sudden and dangerous illness, shall have given an order for medical relief, the said overseer shall forthwith report such case in writing to the relieving officer of the district, or to the board of guardians of the union, and the amount of such relief or the fact of having made such order.

Art. 2. If any overseer of the poor of any parish receive an order under the hands and seals of two justices, according to the provisions of the said act, directing relief to be given to any aged or infirm person, without such person being required to reside in any workhouses, he shall forthwith transmit the same to the relieving officer of the district, to be laid before the guardians at their next meeting, that they may be enabled without delay to give to the relieving officer the necessary directions as to the amount and nature of the relief to be given.

Art. 3. If any overseer receive an order for medical relief from any justice, in case of sudden and dangerous illness, he shall, as soon as may be after complying with such order, report the fact of his having received the same, and the manner in which he has complied with it, in writing to the relieving officer of the district, or to the board of guardians of the union.

Overseers may take credit for all sums properly expended, but not for disbursements to which the poor rate is not properly applicable. If the overseers lawfully, by virtue of their office, contract a debt on account of the parish within three months prior to the

termination of their year of office, and the same has
not been discharged by them before their year of office
is determined, such debt is payable by and recoverable
from the succeeding overseers and chargeable upon the
poor rate.   If the debt was contracted during the year
of office, but more than three months prior to its
termination, it may be paid by their immediate successors if the vestry and the Poor Law board consent.

Overseers wilfully disobeying the legal and reasonable
orders of the justices or guardians, in carrying the rules
of the Local Government board or the provisions of
the New Poor Law Act into execution, are liable, on
conviction before two justices, to pay a fine of not
more than £5.

By the 7 & 8 Vict. c. 101, s. 63, if the overseers
wilfully neglect to make or collect sufficient rates for
the relief of the poor, or to pay such money to the
guardians as they require, and if, by reason of such
neglect, any relief directed by the guardians to be
given be delayed or withheld for seven days, every
such overseer is, upon conviction, to forfeit not exceeding £20.

And by the 12 & 13 Vict. c. 103, s. 7, if the contribution to be made by the overseers to the board of
guardians is in arrear, two justices may, on an application signed by the chairman of the board, summon any
of the overseers, and order the amount to be levied by
distress and sale of their goods.

For the penalties imposed upon overseers fraudulently removing paupers, see the chapter *post*, upon
Removal and Settlement.

Overseers were formerly forbidden, under a penalty

of £100, to supply provisions for the use of the poor of the union or parish, but the prohibition was removed by a recent act.

In addition to their duties in the levying of poor rates and the administration of the poor laws, overseers are also directed (by the 6 Vict. c. 18) to perform various duties in respect of publishing lists of voters and of claims and objections in counties and boroughs.   They are required to attend the revising barrister's court, and are entitled to receive, out of the first moneys to be collected for the relief of the poor of their parish or place, such a sum as is allowed by the certificate of the revising barrister in respect of the expenses incurred by them in carrying the act into effect.   They are also bound to repay to the town clerk of a borough all moneys properly expended by him in relation to the registration of voters, but not any remuneration for his loss of time or services.

CHAPTER XXVII.

OF ASSISTANT OVERSEERS AND COLLECTORS.

THE vestry may nominate assistant overseers, with such salary, to be paid out of the poor rates, as they may deem reasonable; the formal appointment being made by two justices, by warrant under their hand and seal.

The assistant overseer or overseers (for the vestry may appoint one or more) are to perform all the duties of overseers, and continue in office until their appointment is revoked or they resign.

The offices of overseer and of assistant overseer are incompatible. No person, being an overseer of the parish, is qualified to be appointed assistant overseer.

On the application of the guardians of a parish or union, the Local Government board may direct the appointment of a paid collector of rates in such parish or union. The appointment is made by the guardians, and, in fact, immediately such an order as that to which we have just referred has been made by the Local Government board, the power of the vestry or parish officers, or any other persons than the guardians to appoint a collector or assistant overseer ceases, except where they are appointed under a local act for a parish containing above 20,000 inhabitants. All collectors and assistant overseers are (subject to the rules of the Local Government board) to obey in all matters relating to the duties of overseer, the directions of the majority of the overseers for the parish for which they act. They are to give security for the performance of their duties to the guardians or (if there be none) to the overseers.

The vestry of a district for which an assistant overseer or collector has been appointed under the order of the Poor Law board, may, if they will, appoint him to discharge all the duties of an overseer, but this will not discharge the other overseers from their responsibility for the provision and supply of moneys necessary for the relief of the poor, or for any purposes for which poor rates may be made.

The Local Government board have, with respect to assistant overseers and collectors, the same powers which they are authorized, as we shall see by a subsequent chapter, to exercise with reference to the paid officers of the board of guardians.

The duties of a collector are laid down by an order of the Poor Law board, dated the 17th of March, 1847. They are:—To assist the churchwardens in making and levying the poor rates; to collect the rates; to assist in filling up receipts, keeping books, and making returns relating to the rates; to produce the rate and other account books when required; to balance the rates, and to furnish the churchwardens and overseers with a list of defaulters, and under their direction to institute proceedings against them; to attend the meetings of the guardians, and obey the lawful directions of the guardians and of the majority of the overseers. By a subsequent order of the 15th November, 1867, the collector is further required to assist the overseers of the parish for which he acts, in making out and serving the notices of poor rates in arrear required to be made out and served by the Representation of the People Act, 1867.

CHAPTER XXVIII.

OF THE AUDIT OF PARISH AND UNION ACCOUNTS.

THE Poor Law board were, and the Local Government board are, authorized to combine parishes and unions, from time to time, into districts, for the audit of parochial and union accounts, relating to the administration of the poor law. Until 1868, the chairman and vice-chairman of each union in the district elected the auditor, but, in the year we have just mentioned, the power of appointing to any auditorship which might thereafter become vacant, was transferred to the Poor Law board. It is now exercised by the Local Government board.

The auditor has power to examine, audit, allow, or disallow all accounts and items in such accounts relating to moneys applicable to the relief of the poor of the parishes and unions in the district, and to charge any deficiency or loss incurred by the negligence or misconduct of a party accounting, and any sum not brought into account, against such person, and to certify on the face of the accounts any money, books, &c., found to be due from any person. Ratepayers may be present at the audit, and object to the accounts.

Officers or persons who have been duly summoned,* not attending the audit, not producing accounts and vouchers, or not signing such declarations as are required, are liable to penalties.

If the auditor certifies any sum to be due to the union or parish from any officer whose accounts he has audited, in respect of any balance, any payment illegally made by him, or any loss or deficiency occasioned by his negligence or misconduct, he is to report it to the Local Government board; and the person surcharged must pay the sum declared to be due from him to the treasurer of the union within seven days. If he do not, the auditor may proceed to recover the same by proceedings taken before two justices of the

* Fourteen days' notice of the audit must be given to the overseers by the auditor; and it must also be advertised in a newspaper circulating in the county.

county where the treasurer of the union resides.
They have no option but to grant a distress warrant
to enforce the payment, unless the party aggrieved
remove the proceedings by *certiorari* into the Court of
Queen's Bench, which will decide as to the legality of
the surcharge. This court can, however, only decide
according to the strict law of the case. And it is,
therefore, better, when a payment has been made
which, although not strictly legal, is still fair and
reasonable, to take another course, pointed out by
the 11 & 12 Vict. c. 91. Under that act, a party
aggrieved by a surcharge on the part of an auditor
may, in lieu of applying for a *certiorari*, apply to the
Local Government board to inquire into, and decide
upon, the lawfulness of the reasons stated by the
auditor. The board may then make such order
therein as they deem requisite for determining the
question ; and they may decide the same according
to the merits of the case ; and if they find that any
disallowance or surcharge was lawfully made, but that
the subject-matter thereof was incurred under such
circumstances as made it fair and equitable that it
should be remitted, they may, by order, in writing,
under the hand of the president, and countersigned
by a secretary or assistant secretary, direct it to be
remitted, upon payment of the costs (if any) incurred
by the auditor, or other competent authority, in enforcing such disallowance or surcharge.

CHAPTER XXIX.

OF THE UNION OFFICERS.

THE Local Government board are empowered to direct boards of guardians to appoint such paid officers, with such qualifications as they think requisite, for superintending or assisting in the relief or employment of the poor, and for examining and auditing, allowing or disallowing, accounts in the several unions, and for otherwise carrying into execution the acts relative to the relief of the poor. The board are also authorized by the New Poor Law Act to specify, and direct the execution of, the duties of such officers, and the places or limits in which the same are to be performed; to direct the mode of appointment, and determine their continuance in office or dismissal, and the amount and nature of the security to be given by them. They may also regulate the salaries of such officers, and the proportion in which such parishes or unions are to contribute thereto.

By sect. 48 of the same act, the Local Government board may by their order remove the master of any workhouse, assistant overseer, or other paid officer of any parish or union, upon, or without, the suggestion of the overseers or guardians, and may require another to be appointed in his room; and the person so removed shall not be competent to fill any paid office connected with the relief of the poor, without the sanction of the commissioners. And no person shall be eligible to hold any parochial office, or to have the management of the poor in any way, who has been convicted of felony, fraud, or forgery.

Under the powers conferred upon them by this and some other statutes, the Poor Law board issued certain orders, regulating the appointment, qualifications, salaries, &c., of the paid officers of unions, which not only govern these subjects, but furnish the most succinct general view of them. We shall quote the most important articles of the principal order (that of the 24th July, 1847) which relate to these leading points, and are still in force. It would be obviously impossible, in the space at our command, to enter into the duties of each officer, which are specified with great minuteness in the orders of the board, to which those who desire further information must refer for an authoritative statement.

THE APPOINTMENT OF OFFICERS.

The guardians shall, whenever it may be requisite, or whenever a vacancy may occur, appoint fit persons to hold the undermentioned offices, and to perform the duties respectively assigned to them:—1. Clerk to the guardians. 2. Treasurer to the union. 3. Chaplain. 4. Medical officer for the workhouse. 5. District medical officer. 6. Master of the workhouse. 7. Matron of the workhouse. 8. Schoolmaster. 9. Schoolmistress. 10. Porter. 11. Nurse. 12. Relieving officer. 13. Superintendent of out-door labour; and also such assistants as the guardians, with the consent of the commissioners (i. e. at present the Local Government board), may deem necessary for the efficient performance of the duties of any of the said officers, &c.*

The officers so appointed to, or holding any of, the said offices, as well as all persons temporarily discharging the duties of such offices, shall respectively perform such duties as may be required of them by the rules and regulations of the commissioners in force at the time, together with all such other duties conformable with the nature of their respective offices, as the guardians may lawfully require them to perform.

All officers are to be appointed at a meeting of the board of guardians (due notice having been given that the appointment will be made), at which three or more members are present, by a majority of those present; and their appointment is to be immediately notified to the Local Government board.

THE QUALIFICATION OF OFFICERS.

Unless the consent of the Poor Law board † have been previously obtained, no person shall hold the office of clerk, treasurer, master, or relieving officer, under this order, who has not reached the age of twenty-one years; no person shall hold the office of master of

---

* In the consolidated orders issued to unions since 1847, this article proceeds as follows :—" And the said guardians shall, from time to time afterwards, whenever a vacancy may occur, appoint a fit person to supply such vacancy, except in the case of the superintendent of out-door labour, whose office shall be filled as and when the guardians find it requisite to employ such an officer."

† Whenever the words "Poor Law board" occur in these orders, or in our quotations from them, we must now, of course, read "Local Government board."

a workhouse, or matron of a workhouse having no
master, unless he or she be able to keep accounts; no
person shall hold the office of relieving officer unless
he be able to keep accounts, and unless he reside in
the district for which he may be appointed to act,
devote his whole time to the performance of the duties
of his office, and abstain from following any trade or
profession, and from entering into any other service;
no person shall hold the office of nurse who is not
able to read written directions on medicines.

No person shall be appointed to the office of
master, matron, schoolmaster, schoolmistress, porter,
or relieving officer, under this order, who does not
agree to give one month's notice previous to resigning
the office, or to forfeit one month's amount of salary,
to be deducted from the amount of salary due at the
time of such resignation.

No person (except under special circumstances), is
(under an order of the Poor Law board, dated December 10th, 1859) to hold the office of medical officer
unless he is registered under the Medical Act of 1858,
and is qualified by law to practise *both* medicine and
surgery in England and Wales, such qualification
being established by the production to the board of
guardians of a diploma, certificate of a degree, licence,
or other instrument, granted or issued by competent
legal authority *in Great Britain or Ireland,* testifying
to the medical or surgical, or medical and surgical,
qualifications of the candidate for the office. A
diploma or dégree of surgeon, such person having
been in actual practice as an apothecary on the 1st
August, 1815; or a warrant or commission as sur-

geon, or assistant surgeon, or apothecary, in Her
Majesty's army, or as surgeon or assistant surgeon
in the service of the Honourable East India Company,
dated previous to the 1st August, 1826, will also
qualify a person for appointment as a medical officer,
provided he be only registered under the Medical Act,
1858.

No person shall hold the office of chaplain, under
this order, without the consent of the bishop of the
diocese to his appointment, signified in writing.

SALARY AND SECURITY.

The guardians are to pay to the officers or assistants
appointed under this order such salaries or remuneration
as the Local Government board may, from time to time,
direct or approve. Every treasurer, master, matron of
a workhouse in which there is no master, or clerk, and
every other officer whom the guardians shall so require
to do, shall give the bond of two sureties, or of a
guarantee society (expressly authorized by statute),
as security for the faithful performance of their duties.

THE DISMISSAL AND SUSPENSION OF OFFICERS.

The Poor Law board are authorized to suspend or
dismiss any of these officers; and without their consent the guardians can dismiss none but a porter,
nurse, assistant, or servant.

The guardians may, however, at their discretion, suspend from the discharge of his or her duties, any
master, matron, schoolmaster, schoolmistress, medical
officer, relieving officer, or superintendent of outdoor

labour; and the guardians shall, in case of every such suspension, forthwith report the same, together with the cause thereof, to the commissioners; and if the commissioners remove the suspension of such officer by the guardians, he or she shall forthwith resume the performance of his or her duties.

If any officer or assistant appointed to or holding any office or employment under this order, be at any time prevented, by sickness or accident, or other sufficient reason, from the performance of his duties, the guardians may a point a fit person to act as his temporary substitute, and may pay him a reasonable compensation for his services; and every such appointment shall be reported to the commissioners as soon as the same shall have been made.

When any officer may die, resign, or become legally disqualified to perform the duties of his office, the guardians shall, as soon as conveniently may be after such death, resignation, or disqualification, give notice thereof to the commissioners, and proceed to make a new appointment to the office so vacant, in the manner prescribed by the above regulations.

In every case not otherwise provided for by this order, every officer shall perform his duties in person, and shall not entrust the same to a deputy, except with the special permission of the commissioners on the application of the guardians.

SUPERANNUATION OF OFFICERS.

The guardians of any union or parish, and the trustees or overseers of any parish incorporated under a local act, may now, with the consent of the Local

Government board, grant to any officer whose whole time has been devoted to the service of the union or parish, and who has become incapable of discharging the duties of his office with efficiency by reason of permanent infirmity of mind or body, or of old age, upon his resigning or otherwise ceasing to hold his office, an annual allowance, not in any case exceeding two-thirds of his then salary, whether computed according to a fixed sum, or to a poundage; and such superannuation allowance is to be charged to the same fund as that to which the salary would have been charged if the person had remained in office.

No grant of a superannuation allowance is, however, to be made without one month's previous notice in writing being given to every guardian, &c., of the union or parish of the proposal to make such grant, and of the time when it is to be brought forward.

No officer is to be entitled to a superannuation allowance on the ground of age, unless he has completed the full age of sixty years, and has served as an officer of some union or parish for twenty years at least.*

To a medical officer, the guardians may, with the assent of the Local Government board, grant a superannuation allowance, *notwithstanding that he has not devoted his whole time to the union or parish.*

* See on the subject of the superannuation of officers, the 27 & 28 Vict. c. 421, the 29 & 30 Vict. c. 113, the 30 & 31 Vict. c. 106, and the 33 & 34 Vict. c. 94.

CHAPTER XXX.

OF THE RELIEF OF THE POOR.

THE destitute poor are relieved at the expense of
and in the union where they are settled, or from which
they are irremovable.*   The funds necessary for
the purpose are furnished by the overseers of the
several parishes, who provide, by laying rates, the
sums required for the purpose by the board of guardians of the union, or by the select vestry in cases
where the administration of the poor law is vested in
such a body by any local act.   The cost of relief is
now charged upon what is called the "common fund"
of the union, *i. e.* a fund to which each parish of the
union contributes in proportion to its assessment.
Out of the same fund is also defrayed the cost of the
relief given to any poor person becoming chargeable
to a union, being a destitute wayfarer or wanderer or
foundling,† as well as the cost of burial of such person
dying within the union.

The administration of the relief is under the direction of the board of guardians of the union, or of the
select vestry (when such a body exists), but it must

* As to Settlement and Irremovability, see Chapter XXXII.,
post.

† This extends to a destitute child under the age of twelve,
who is deserted by both parents, or by its surviving parent, and
who is not in the care or custody of some relative, guardian, or
friend, and whose settlement is not known.

P

take place subject to and in accordance with any rules and regulations which the Local Government board may issue upon the subject. There are, indeed, certain special cases in which relief may be given or ordered by the overseers and justices of the peace, which will be found noticed in the chapters devoted to these officers.

And while *destitute paupers* are entitled to relief, it has been enacted by the 12 & 13 Vict. c. 103, s. 16 (in order to provide against persons improperly becoming chargeable), that when a pauper has in his possession or belonging to him any money or valuable security, the guardians of the union or parish within which he is chargeable may take and appropriate so much of such money or the produce of such security, or recover the same as a debt before any local court, as will reimburse them for the amount expended by them, whether on behalf of the common fund or of any parish, in the relief of such pauper during twelve months prior to such taking and appropriation, or proceeding for the recovery thereof (as the case may be) ; and in the event of the death of any pauper having in his possession or belonging to him any money or property, the guardians of the union or parish wherein he dies may reimburse themselves the expenses incurred by them in and about the burial of such pauper and his maintenance at any time during the twelve months previous to his decease.

The leading division of persons requiring relief is into —impotent and able-bodied poor. The impotent poor are such as, from age or physical disability, are unable to work ; the able-bodied are such as are not subject to such incapacity. The former may be relieved by the guardians, at their discretion, either in the workhouse or by out-door relief.

The relief of the able-bodied poor is regulated minutely by the orders of the Poor Law board, from which, however, the overseers or guardians may, in cases of emergency, depart, with the approval of the commissioners. The following is the the order (dated December 21, 1844) with respect to the relief of such persons in unions which have provided adequate workhouse accommodation.

Art. I. Every able-bodied person, male or female, requiring relief from any parish within any of the said unions shall be relieved wholly in the workhouse of the said union, together with such of the family of every such able-bodied person as may be resident with him or her and may not be in employment, and together with the wife of any such able-bodied male person, if she be resident with him; save and except in the following cases :—

1st. Where such person shall require relief on account of sudden and urgent necessity.

2nd. Where such person shall require relief on account of any sickness, accident, or bodily or mental infirmity affecting such person or any of his or her family.

3rd. Where such person shall require relief for the purpose of defraying the expenses, either wholly or in part, of the burial of his or her family.

4th. Where such person, being a widow, shall be in the first six months of her widowhood.

5th. Where such person shall be a widow, and have

a legitimate child or children dependent upon her and incapable of earning his, her, or their livelihood, and no illegitimate child born after the commencement of her widowhood.

6th. Where such person shall be confined in any gaol or place of safe custody.

7th. Where such person shall be the wife or child of any able-bodied man who shall be in the service of Her Majesty as a soldier, sailor, or marine.

8th. Where any able-bodied person, not being a soldier, sailor, or marine, shall not reside within the union, but the wife, child, or children of such person shall reside within the same, the board of guardians, according to their discretion, may afford relief in the workhouse to such wife, child, or children, or may allow out-door relief for any such child or children being within the age of nurture and resident with the mother within the union.

Art. II. In every case in which out-door relief shall be given on account of sickness, accident, or infirmity to any member of the family of any able-bodied male person resident within any of the said unions, or to any member of the family of any able-bodied male person, an extract from the medical officer's weekly report (if any such officer shall have attended the case), stating the nature of such weakness, accident, or infirmity, shall be specially entered in the minutes of the proceedings of the board of guardians of the day on which the relief is ordered or subsequently allowed. But if the board of guardians shall think fit, a certificate, under the hand of the medical officer of the union, or of the medical practitioner in attendance on the party, shall be laid before the board, stating the nature of such sickness, accident, or infirmity, and a copy of the same shall be in like manner entered in the minutes.

Art. III. No relief shall be given from the poor rates of any parish comprised in any of the said unions to any person who does not reside in some place within the union ; save and except in the following cases :—

1st. Where such person being casually within such parish shall become destitute.

2nd. Where such person shall require relief on account of any sickness, accident, or bodily or mental infirmity affecting such person or any of his or her family.

3rd. Where such person shall be entitled to receive relief from any parish in which he may not be resident under any order which justices may by law be authorized to make.

4th. Where such person, being a widow, shall be in the first six months of her widowhood.

5th. Where such person is a widow who has a legitimate child dependent on her for support, and no illegitimate child born after the commencement of her widowhood, and who, at the time of her husband's death, was resident with him in some place other than the parish of her legal settlement, and not situate in the union in which such parish may be comprised.

6th. Where such person shall be a child under the age of sixteen, maintained in a workhouse or establishment for the education of pauper children, and not situate within the union.

7th. Where such person shall be the wife or child, residing within the union, of some person not able-bodied and not residing within the union.

8th. Where such person shall have been in the receipt of relief from some parish in the union at some time within the twelve calendar months next preceding the date of the order, being settled in such parish, and not resident within the union.

Art. IV. Where the husband of any woman is beyond the seas, or in custody of the law, or in confinement in a licensed house or asylum as a lunatic or idiot, all relief which the guardians give to his wife or her children shall be given to such woman in the same manner and subject to the same conditions as if she were a widow.

The following order regulates the administration of relief in unions unprovided with adequate* workhouse accommodation.

Art. I. Whenever the guardians allow relief to any able-bodied male person out of the workhouse, one-half, at least, of the relief so allowed shall be given in articles of food or fuel, or in other articles of absolute necessity.

Art. II. In any case in which the guardians allow relief for a longer period than one week to an indigent poor person, resident within their union or parish, without requiring that such person shall be received into the workhouse, such relief shall be given or administered weekly, or at such more frequent periods as they deem expedient.

* Adequate, that is, to the reception of all persons at the time requiring relief.

Art. III. It shall not be lawful for the guardians, or their officers, to establish any applicant for relief in trade or business; nor to redeem from pawn, for any such applicant, any tools, implements, or articles; nor to purchase and give him any tools, &c., except articles of clothing or bedding when urgently needed, and such articles as are mentioned in *Art.* I.; nor to pay, directly or indirectly, the expense of his conveyance (except in certain cases); nor to give money to or on his account for the purpose of effecting any of the above objects; nor to pay, wholly or in part, the rent of his house or lodging, nor to apply any portion of the relief ordered in payment of such rent; but this article does not apply to any shelter or temporary lodging procured for a poor person in case of sudden or urgent necessity or mental imbecility.

Art. IV. is in effect the same as *Art.* III. of the order just quoted, relating to the relief of paupers in places where there is adequate workhouse accommodation.

Art. V. No relief shall be given to any able-bodied male person while he is employed for wages or other hire or remuneration by any person.

Art. VI. Every able-bodied male person, if relieved out of the workhouse, shall be set to work by the guardians, and be kept employed under their direction and superintendence so long as he continues to receive relief.

Art. VII. contains exceptions to the preceding articles similar to those contained in the first article of the previous order.

Art. X. If the guardians shall, upon consideration of the special circumstances of any particular case, deem it expedient to depart from any of the above regulations (except *Art.* III.), and within twenty-one days report the same and the grounds thereof to the Poor Law board, the relief given before an answer to their report has been returned shall not be deemed to be contrary to the provisions of this order; and if the Poor Law board approve of such departure, and notify such approval to the guardians, all relief given after such notification in accordance with such approval shall be lawful.

The guardians may give any relief sanctioned by these orders, *by way of loan* (orders of December 21, 1844, and December 14, 1852), and provision is made for the recovery thereof, either by proceedings before two justices (11 & 12 Vict. c. 43, s. 90), or in the county court (11 & 12 Vict. c. 110, s. 8).

Although the guardians must, in the first instance, relieve all destitute poor persons chargeable to the union or any parish thereof, any relief given to such persons as are "old, blind, lame, or impotent or unable to work," may be recovered, either wholly or in part, by the order of two justices, from the parents, the grandfathers or grandmothers, or the children of such persons, if these are able to pay it. But no relief given to persons who are able to work can be recovered from their relations. If any person who is liable refuses to pay any sum so assessed upon him by the justices, he is liable to a penalty of 20s. a month, and may also be indicted.

Husbands are bound to maintain their wives, and fathers or mothers their children, if they are able. And if a husband, father, or mother absconds from his or her place of abode, leaving any wife or child chargeable to the poor rates, such deserters may be punished as rogues and vagabonds, and any goods, profits of land, &c., of which they may be in possession, or to which they may be entitled, may be seized, by order of two justices, and (after confirmation of the order by the sessions) may be disposed of to reimburse the parish for providing for such wife, &c.

If relief is given to any Greenwich or Chelsea pensioner, or to any one he was bound to maintain, the secretary at war may order such relief to be repaid out of his pension, but so that it shall not exceed one-half of his pension, when it has been advanced to his wife *or* one child whom he is bound to maintain, nor more than two-thirds of such pension when advanced to his wife *and* one or more such children. The whole of his pension may be absorbed in the repayment of relief granted to *himself.*

We ought, perhaps, here to notice briefly the law with respect to the maintenance of one class of persons—illegitimate children. The mother of any such child, so long as she is unmarried or a widow, is bound to maintain it until it attains the age of sixteen. She may, indeed, obtain aid from the putative father under an order of affiliation; and after her death, or if she be incapacitated, and the child then become chargeable to the parish from the neglect of the putative father to make the payments mentioned in the order, the guardians may enforce the order in the same way as the mother might have done, and may obtain from the justices an order for the payment of the allowance awarded by the affiliation order to such relieving or other officer of the union

as they may appoint. And it must be remarked, that a
man marrying a woman having an illegitimate child, is
bound to maintain it as part of his family until it attains
the age of sixteen, or until the death of its mother. And
the marriage of the latter relieves the putative father,
during her life and that of her husband, from all
liability under any order of affiliation which may have
been made upon him.

Poor persons may be enabled or assisted to emigrate
under the following conditions :—

1st. The overseers and ratepayers of any parish duly
convened may, subject to the approval of the Local
Government board, direct that a sum of money not
exceeding half the annual poor rate for the previous
three years shall be raised or borrowed (in the latter
case it must be repayable in a period not exceeding
five years), out of or upon the security of the poor
rates, in aid of any fund or contribution for defraying
the expenses of the emigration of poor persons settled
in the parish. And such fund, when raised, must be
applied in accordance with the rules and orders of the
Poor Law board (4 & 5 Will. 4, c. 76, s. 62).

2nd. Guardians may, with the consent of the Local
Government board, and in accordance with these regulations, procure or assist in procuring the emigration
of persons rendered irremovable by the 9 & 10 Vict.
c. 66 and subsequent statutes (see *post*, Chapter
XXXII.), the cost to be charged upon the common
fund of the union (11 & 12 Vict. c. 110, s. 5).

3rd. The guardians may, with the order and subject
to the rules of the Local Government board, and without the assent of a meeting of ratepayers and over-

seers, expend not more than £10 each in promoting
the emigration of poor persons settled in a parish of
the union ; such sum to be charged to the parish of
settlement, but not to be expended without the consent of
the guardian (or, if more than one, the majority of the
guardians) of that parish (12 & 13 Vict. c. 103, s. 20).

4th. Guardians are empowered, subject to the orders
and rules mentioned in the last paragraph, to defray
the cost of the emigration of poor orphans or deserted
children having no settlement, or whose settlement is
unknown, but who are chargeable to the union.   As
they are chargeable to the common fund of the union,
the assent of the guardians of any particular parish
will not be necessary.   The consent of the orphan,
signified before the justices in petty sessions, is necessary before his emigration can take place.

The guardians of certain unions, mentioned in the
schedule to an order issued by the Poor Law board on the
25th November, 1870, may board-out pauper children in
homes beyond the limits of their own district, provided
that they have entered into arrangements, approved by
the Local Government board, with two or more persons
called the boarding-out committee, for the purpose of
finding and superintending such houses. Although the
operation of this order is at present confined to a
certain (but considerable) number of unions, there is
no doubt that any union from which it might be really
desirable to board-out children, would have little difficulty in getting included in it.*

* The exercise of this power of boarding-out is subject to
numerous and minute conditions and regulations, for which
we must refer to the order itself.

The guardians may, under the control and subject to the rules, &c., of the Local Government board, let allotments of land to poor persons, but it is sufficient to allude to their possession of the power, as it is never, or hardly ever, put in operation. It is more important to state the provisions of the 18 & 19 Vict. c. 34, which enables the guardians to grant relief for the purpose of enabling any poor person lawfully relieved out of the workhouse to provide education for any child between the ages of four and sixteen, in any school to be approved of by the guardians for such time and under such conditions as they see fit. Under the 25 & 26 Vict. c. 43, the guardians may also send any poor child to a school duly certified by the Poor Law board, and supported either wholly or partially by voluntary subscriptions, the managers of which shall be willing to receive such child ; and they may pay for the maintenance, clothing, and education of such child (not exceeding the total sum which would have been charged for the maintenance of such child if relieved in the workhouse during the same period), and for his or her conveyance to or from school, and in the case of death the expenses of his or her burial.

We have now to speak of a particular class of poor persons, called *casual poor*. "Casual poor," in the words of a writer on the subject, "are those who in consequence of accident, calamity, or any other circumstance, require immediate parochial relief, and thus become a burthen upon the funds of the parish in which they may happen to be at the time when the necessity for such relief arises, although their settlement is elsewhere. The parish officers must relieve

them, and they are not removable to their legal settlement while detained by the effect of such accident, &c.;
nor can the relief given to the casual poor be recovered
from the parish to which they belong, or from any
others than the parish where they are, even in the case
of continued illness, unless such parish or persons have
expressly promised to pay."

We can only briefly notice the subject of pauper
lunatics; referring those who desire further information to the " Lunatic Asylum Act, 1853."* Under
that act, pauper lunatics resident in a union, or being
wandering and at large there, who are proper persons
to be sent to an asylum, are to be sent there by the
guardians, the order of a justice being first obtained,
and being founded upon proper medical testimony.
But nothing in the act (sect. 68) is to prevent any
relation or friend from keeping such lunatic under
his own care, if he satisfies the justices or the visitors
of the asylum in which the lunatic is intended to be
placed that he will be properly taken care of. The
cost of maintaining a pauper lunatic in an asylum is
to be defrayed by any union in which he was settled
or from which he was irremovable at the time of his
being sent to the asylum; or if he is in neither of
these categories, then his maintenance is to be charged
to the county or borough rate of the county or
borough in which he was found. On the other hand,
the guardians of any union may (31 & 32 Vict. c. 122,
s. 43), with the consent of the Local Government
board and the commissioners in lunacy, receive into
the workhouse any chronic lunatic not being danger-

* 16 & 17 Vict. c. 97.

ous (who may have been removed to a lunatic asylum, and selected by the superintendent of the asylum, and certified by him to be fit and proper so to be removed), upon such terms as may be agreed upon between the guardians and the committee or visitors of the asylum.

The guardians may provide for the reception, maintenance, and instruction of any adult pauper being blind or deaf and dumb, in any hospital or institution established for the reception of persons suffering under such infirmities, and may pay the charges incurred in the conveyance of such pauper to and from the institution, as well as those incurred in his maintenance, support, and instruction. They may also send children of the same unfortunate classes to appropriate schools.

CHAPTER XXXI.

OF THE WORKHOUSE.

UNDER the New Poor Law Act and subsequent statutes the Poor Law board originally, and now the Local Government board may, by writing under their hand and seal, with the consent in writing of a majority of the guardians of any union, or of a majority of the ratepayers and overseers entitled to vote in any parish, order the overseers or guardians of any parish or union not having a workhouse, to build one.* And

---

* In the case of certain parishes, where the relief of the poor is administered under the 22 Geo. 3, or under local acts, the Local Government board have now (under the 31 & 32 Vict. c. 122) power to order the erection of a workhouse without the consent mentioned in the text.

with such consent, they may direct any existing workhouse to be enlarged or altered. They may, indeed,
order by their own authority, any alteration or enlargement of a workhouse the cost of which shall not exceed one-tenth of the average annual amount of the
rates raised for the relief of the poor in such parish or
union for three years ending the Easter next preceding
the raising of such money. The overseers or guardians
may borrow the money necessary for such erection or
alteration, and may charge the future poor rates of
the parish or union with the amount of the money
borrowed. The principal sum, whether raised within
the year or borrowed, is in no case to exceed two-
thirds of the aggregate amount of poor rates raised
during the three years ending at the Easter next
preceding the raising of such money (but when the
site is within any municipal borough, or without five
miles from the outward boundary thereof, the cost
of such site may be added*), and any loan or money
borrowed for such purposes must be repaid by annual
instalments of not less than one-twentieth of the sum
borrowed, with interest for the same, in any one year.
Workhouses, or other property of a poor-law union,
may be sold or exchanged by and with the concurrence
of the authorities in whom is vested the power of
building or enlarging a workhouse. And the guardians may, with the consent of the Local Government
board, hire or take on lease, temporarily or for a term

* The guardians of any parish or union, any part of which
is within the metropolitan police district, and the vestry of the
parish of Liverpool, are, by the 7 & 8 Vict. c. 101, s. 30, re-
leased from this restriction.

of years not exceeding five, any land or building for the purposes of the relief of the poor and the use of the guardians or their officers.

When the workhouse of any union or parish is governed by the rules and orders of the Poor Law or Local Government board, the guardians of the union or parish to which it belongs may in the case of the over-crowding of the workhouse of any other union or parish, or the prevalence or any reasonable apprehension of any epidemic or contagious disease, or in or towards carrying out any legal resolution for the emigration of poor persons, with the consent of the Local Government board, receive, lodge, and maintain in the first-mentioned workhouse, upon terms to be mutually agreed upon by the respeetive boards of guardians, any poor person belonging to such other parish or union. And when in any union or parish there is a workhouse or building having adequate provision for the reception, maintenance and education of poor children, and there is more accommodation therein at any time than the guardians of such union or parish require for the poor children of their own union or parish, such guardians may, with the consent of the Local Government board, contract with the guardians of any other union or parish, any part of which is not more than twenty miles from such workhouse, for the reception, maintenance, and instruction therein of any poor children under the age of 16, chargeable to such other union or parish, or to any parish in such union, being orphans, or deserted by their parents, or whose parents or surviving parent consent.

Workhouses are to be conducted and managed in

accordance with such rules, orders, and regulations as the Local Government board may from time to time make upon the subject. Those at present in existence contain provisions both numerous and minute. We can here only offer a summary of the most important points.

Paupers are to be admitted in some one of the following modes *only :*—By a written or printed order of the board of guardians, signed by their clerk. By a provisional, written, or printed order, signed by a relieving officer or an overseer. By the master of the workhouse (or during his absence, or inability to act, by the matron), without any order, in any case of sudden or urgent necessity. Provided, however, that the master may admit any pauper delivered at the workhouse under an order of removal to a parish in the union. No pauper is to be admitted if the order for his admission bears date more than six days before its presentation.

On admission, paupers are to be thoroughly cleansed; and are also to be submitted to the examination of the medical officer, in order that, if necessary, they may be placed in the sick or lunatic wards. No greater number are to be admitted into any ward than are, from time to time, sanctioned by the Local Government board.

The paupers are, as far as possible, to be classed as follows, each class being kept in a separate ward :—

Class I. Men infirm through age or any other cause.

Class II. Able-bodied men, and youths above the age of fifteen years.

Class III. Boys above the age of seven and under that of fifteen.

Class IV. Women infirm through age or any other cause.

Class V. Able-bodied women, and girls above the age of fifteen.

Class VI. Girls above the age of seven years and under that of fifteen.

Class VII. Children under seven years of age.

The guardians are, so far as circumstances will admit, to subdivide any of these classes with reference to the moral character or behaviour or the previous habits of the inmates, or to such other grounds as may seem expedient.

Nothing in this order is to compel the guardians to separate any married couple, both being paupers of the first and fourth classes respectively, provided the guardians shall set apart for the exclusive use of every such couple a sleeping apartment, separate from that of the other paupers. And by the 10 & 11 Vict. c. 109, s. 23, when two persons, being husband and wife, both of whom are above the age of sixty years, are received into a workhouse, they are not to be compelled to live separate and apart from each other.

Paupers of certain classes may be employed in attending upon or superintending those of others.

Casual poor wayfarers admitted by the master or matron, are to be kept in a separate ward of the workhouse, which the guardians are required to provide in such manner and to furnish in such a way as the Local Government board may direct. They must also be admitted, dieted, set to work, and discharged in conformity with the regulations prescribed by the Local Government board.

The inmates of the workhouse must be dieted with the food and in the manner described in the dietary table which may be prescribed for the use of the work-house, and no pauper is to have or consume any liquor or any food or provision other than is allowed in the said dietary table, except on Christmas-day or by the direction of the medical officer, who is authorized to direct such diet as he may deem requisite for any pauper. And if any pauper requires the master or matron to weigh the allowance of provisions served out at any meal, the master or matron shall forthwith weigh such allowance in the presence of the pauper complaining and of two other persons.

The clothing to be worn by the paupers in the workhouse is to be made of such materials as the board of guardians may determine.

The paupers of the several classes shall be kept employed according to their capacity and ability; and the boys and girls who are inmates of the workhouse must, for three of the working hours at least every day, be instructed in reading, writing, arithmetic, and the principles of the Christian religion, and such other instruction must also be imparted to them as may fit them for service and train them to habits of usefulness, industry, and virtue.

The "religious difficulty" in workhouses is now met by a series of clauses in the 31 & 32 Vict. c. 122, which we shall give in full in consequence of the interest attaching to the subject, and the disputes to which it frequently gives rise :—

Sec. 16. The officer for the time being acting as the master of a workhouse, or as the master or superintendent of a district or other pauper school, shall keep a register of the religious creed of the pauper inmates of such work-

Q 2

house or school separate from all other registers, in such form and with such particulars as shall be prescribed by the Poor Law board,* by an order under their seal, and shall, as regards every inmate of such workhouse or school, at the date to be fixed by such order, and subsequently upon the admission of every inmate therein, make due inquiry into the religious creed of such inmate, and enter such religious creed in such register.

Sec. 17. In regard to any child in the workhouse or school under the age of 12 years, whether either of its parents be in the workhouse or not, or whether it be an orphan or deserted child, the master or superintendent shall enter in such register as to the religious creed of such child, the religious creed of the father, if the master or superintendent know, or can ascertain the same by reasonable inquiry, or if the same cannot be so ascertained, the creed of the mother of such child, if the same be known to the said master or superintendent, or can be by him in like manner ascertained ; and the creed of an illegitimate child under the said age shall be deemed to be that of its mother, when that can be ascertained.

Sec. 18. If any question shall arise as to the correctness of any entry in such register, the Poor Law board may, if they think fit, inquire into the circumstances of the case, and determine such question by directing such entry to remain or be amended, according to their judgment.

Sec. 19. Every minister of any denomination officiating in the church, chapel, or other registered place of religious worship of such denomination which shall be nearest to any workhouse or school, or any ratepayer of any parish in the union, shall be allowed to inspect the register which contains the entry of the religious creed of the inmates, at any time of any day, except Sunday, between the hours of ten before noon and four after noon.

---

* Whenever the words " Poor Law board " occur in these clauses, we must now read " Local Government board."

Sec. 20. Such minister may, in accordance with such regulations as the said board shall approve of, or by their order prescribe, visit, and instruct any inmate of such workhouse or school entered in such register or belonging to the same religious creed as such minister belongs to, unless such inmate, being above the age of 14, and after having been visited at least once by such minister, shall object to be instructed by him.

Sec. 21. Every inmate for whom a religious service according to his own creed shall not be provided in the workhouse, shall be permitted, subject to regulations to be approved of or ordered by the Poor Law board, to attend at such times as the said board shall allow, some place of worship of his own denomination within a convenient distance of the said workhouse, if there be such, in the opinion of the board : Provided that the guardians may, for abuse of such permission previously granted, or on some other special ground, refuse permission to any particular inmate, and shall in such case cause an entry of such refusal, and the grounds thereof, to be made in their minutes.

Sec. 22. No child, being an inmate of a workhouse or such school as aforesaid, who shall be regularly visited by a minister of his own religious creed for the purpose of religious instruction, shall, if the parents or surviving parent of such child, or in the case of orphans or deserted children, if such minister make request in writing to that effect, be instructed in any other religious creed, or be required or permitted to attend the service of any other religious creed than that entered in such register as aforesaid, except any child above the age of 12 years who shall desire to receive instruction in some other creed, or to attend the service of any other religious creed, and who shall be considered by the Poor Law board competent to exercise a judgment on the subject.

Sec. 23. The act of the 25 & 26 Vict. c. 43, and sec. 14 of the Poor Law Amendment Act of 1866,* shall apply to

* As to the first of these enactments, see *ante*, p. 183. The

illegitimate as well as to legitimate children ; and with
regard to illegitimate children, the consent of the
mother, if she has the care, custody, or possession of
the child, shall be sufficient for the purposes of these
acts ; and in case of a deserted child or an orphan
child, on behalf of whom no relative, next of kin,
step-parent, or god-parent shall make application, the
poor-law board may exercise the power conferred upon
them by sect. 14 of the said act of 1866, upon being
satisfied that there is reasonable ground for so doing.

In the absence of any order to the contrary by the
board of guardians, any pauper may quit the workhouse upon giving to the master or (during his absence
or inability to act) the matron, a reasonable notice of
his wish to do so ; and in the event of any able-bodied
pauper having a family so quitting the house, the
whole of such family shall be sent with him, unless
the guardians shall, for any special reason, otherwise

---

second is as follows :—"That if the parent, step-parent,
nearest adult male relative, or next of kin of any child not
belonging to the established church, relieved in a workhouse
or in a district school, or in case there should be no parent,
step-parent, nearest adult relative, or next of kin, then the
god-parent of such cnild, makes application to the said board
[*i. e.*, the Local Government board], in that behalf, the board
may, if they think fit, order that such child shall be sent to
some school established for the reception, maintenance, and
education of children of the religion to which such child shall
be found to belong, and duly certified by the Poor Law board
under the statute 25 & 26 Vict. c. 43, and the guardians of
the union to which such child shall be chargeable, shall, according to the terms of such order, cause the child to be conveyed
to such school, and pay the costs and charges of the maintenance, lodging, clothing, and education of the said child
therein, and all the provisions of the said statute shall forthwith apply to the said child."

direct, and such directions shall be in conformity with the regulations of the commissioners with respect to relief in force at the time. But under the 34 & 35 Vict. c. 108, s. 4,* the guardians of any union may direct that any pauper inmate of the workhouse, or the paupers of any class therein, shall be detained in the workhouse, after giving notice to quit the same, for times not exceeding the limited periods hereinafter mentioned, that is to say :—

1. If the pauper has not previously discharged himself from the workhouse within one month before giving the notice, twenty-four hours ;

2. If he has discharged himself once or oftener within such month, forty-eight hours ;

3. If he has discharged himself more than twice within two months before giving the notice, seventy-two hours.

A casual pauper is not entitled to discharge himself from a casual ward before eleven o'clock in the morning on the day following his admission, nor before he has performed the work prescribed for him ; and where a casual pauper has been admitted on more than two occasions during one month into any casual ward of the same union,† he is not entitled to discharge himself before nine o'clock in the morning of the third day after his admission, and he may at any time during that interval be removed by any officer of the guardians, or by a police constable, to the workhouse of the union, and be required to remain in such work-

* This section does not apply to casual paupers.

† Every casual ward of the metropolis is deemed a casual ward of the same union (34 & 35 Vict. c. 108, s. 5).

house for the remainder of the period of his detention.

Any pauper who—(1) absconds or escapes from
or leaves any casual ward before he is entitled to discharge himself therefrom; or (2) refuses to be removed to any workhouse or asylum under the provisions of this act; or (3) absconds or escapes from
or leaves any workhouse or asylum during the period
for which he may be detained therein; or (4) refuses
or neglects, whilst an inmate of any casual ward,
workhouse, or asylum, to do the work or observe the
regulations prescribed; or (5) wilfully gives a false
name, or makes a false statement for the purpose of
obtaining relief, is deemed an idle and disorderly person within the meaning of sect. 3 of the 5 Geo. 4,
c. 83. And every pauper who—(1) commits any of
the offences before mentioned after having been previously convicted as an idle and disorderly person; or
(2) wilfully destroys or injures his own clothes, or
damages any of the property of the guardians, is
deemed a rogue and vagabond within the meaning of
sect. 4 of the same act. The master or porter of
the workhouse may, without any warrant, take such
offending pauper before a magistrate, who is authorized
to punish him by fine or imprisonment on summary
conviction.

No work except the necessary household work and
cooking shall be performed by the inmates of a workhouse on Sunday, Good Friday, and Christmas-day.

Prayers shall be read before breakfast and after
supper every day, and divine service shall be performed
every Sunday in the workhouse (unless the guardians,

with the consent of the local government board, otherwise direct), at which all the paupers shall attend,
except the sick, persons of unsound mind, the young
children, and such as are too infirm to do so; provided
that those paupers who may object so to attend on
account of their professing religious principles differ-
ing from those of the established church, shall also be
exempt from attendance.

Disorderly and refractory paupers are to be punished
by alteration of diet or confinement. The confinement
is only to be inflicted by order of the guardians, unless
the refractory conduct is accompanied with certain
circumstances of aggravation, when the master of the
workhouse may, on his own authority, place a pauper
in confinement for not more than twelve hours.

No corporal punishment shall be inflicted upon
adults of either sex, upon female children, or upon
male children above the age of fourteen. Nor shall
corporal punishment be inflicted upon any other male
child, except by the schoolmaster or master of the
workhouse.

The introduction of spirits or fermented liquor into
a workhouse, either by a pauper or any other person,
without the order in writing of the master, is punishable, on conviction before the justices, with fine or
imprisonment.

Paupers absconding with clothes, the property of
the guardians, may also be imprisoned.

We have already seen (see *ante*, Chapter XXV.) that
the justices of the peace have the power to visit and
inspect workhouses. But in addition to this, it is directed by the rules and orders of the Poor Law board,

that the guardians shall appoint one or more visiting committees from their own body; and each of such committees shall carefully examine the workhouse or workhouses of the union, once in every week at the least; inspect the last reports of the chaplain and medical officer; examine the stores; afford, so far as is practicable, to the inmates an opportunity of making any complaints, and investigate any complaints that may be made to them.

The guardians are, once at least in every year, and as often as may be necessary for cleanliness, to cause all the rooms, wards, offices, and privies belonging to the workhouse to be limewashed. And they are to cause the workhouse, and all its furniture and appurtenances, to be kept in good and substantial repair; and, from time to time, to remedy without delay any such defect in the repair of the house, its drainage, warmth, or ventilation, or in the furniture or fixtures thereof, as may tend to injure the health of the inmates.

CHAPTER XXXII.

OF SETTLEMENT AND REMOVAL.

Part I.—Settlements.

" A SETTLEMENT is the right acquired in any one of the modes pointed out by the poor laws to become a recipient of the benefit of those laws in that parish or place which provides for its own poor, where the right has been last acquired." *   Until the year 1865, the

* Steer's Parish Law, by Hodgson, p. 627.

place to which a pauper was chargeable, and in which he had a right to relief, was the *parish* where he had gained his settlement in the manner we shall presently proceed to explain.   In that year, however, an act (28 & 29 Vict. c. 79) was passed, which enlarged the area of chargeability from the parish to the union. Although a pauper is still, in strictness, settled in a particular parish, the cost of his relief or maintenance is borne by the union, upon the common fund of which it is imposed, as we have already seen.   For most practical purposes, therefore, he may be said to be settled in a union; and, as we shall presently see, he can only be removed from the union where he resides when he becomes chargeable, when the parish of his settlement is in some other union.   He is, then, removed from union to union, and not, as before the year 1865, from parish to parish.

A settlement is acquired—1. By birth.   2. By parentage.   3. By marriage.   4. By apprenticeship. 5. By hiring and by service.   6. By renting a tenement.   7. By payment of rates.   8. By an estate. 9. By serving an office.

1. *By birth.*—Every person is *primâ facie* entitled to a settlement in the place where he is born.   But this he only retains until he is proved to have another, derived from his parents, or acquires one for himself in any of the modes we shall presently describe.   Illegitimate children born before the 14th August, 1834, indeed, were not entitled to derive a settlement from their parents.   But by the New Poor Law Act, those born after that date follow the settlement of their mother until they are sixteen years of age.   They

afterwards return to the settlement of the place of their birth, unless they have, in the meantime, acquired one for themselves.

2. *By parentage.*—Every child born in wedlock acquires, in the first instance, its father's then settlement, if that can be traced; if that cannot be done, the child is entitled to the settlement which its mother had before she married. If neither of these settlements can be traced, then of course the child will be settled in the place of its birth. Supposing the child to have gained the settlement of one of its parents, it follows that, whatever changes it may undergo while the child is yet "unemancipated," and has not acquired any settlement of its own; or if it have in the first instance acquired the settlement of its father, it follows the changes of that so long as he lives, and then, if the mother survive him, it is subsequently governed by hers.

To this, indeed, there is one exception. We shall see presently, that if a mother having become a widow marries again, she obtains the settlement of her second husband, but the settlement of the children by her first marriage is not affected thereby. A child is considered "emancipated" at the age of twenty-one (unless he is an idiot); but he may also be emancipated before that age, either by acquiring a settlement for himself (we shall see presently how a minor may do this), or by assuming a relation, such as that of marriage, or enlistment in Her Majesty's forces (while service continues), which excludes the parental control. When a child is emancipated, it retains that settlement of its parent which it possessed at the time of emancipation, until it acquires one for itself.

3. *By marriage.*—The following are the rules gene-rally applicable to settlements by marriage:—1. A woman marrying a man with a known settlement shall follow it, even whether she lived there with him or not. 2. A wife cannot gain a new settlement for her-self during coverture, or complete one which her hus-band did not live long enough to obtain. 3. A woman marrying a man without a known settlement retains her maiden settlement.

4. *By apprenticeship.*—This settlement is created by the 3 & 4 William and Mary, c. 11, s. 8, which enacts that "if any person shall be bound an apprentice by indenture according to law, viz., for seven years, and inhabit in any town or parish, such binding and inhabiting shall be adjudged a good settlement."

A child cannot be bound apprentice under the age of seven. All indentures apprenticing a child to a chimney-sweeper under the age of eight years are void; and we have already seen that no child can be bound apprentice by parish officers till the age of nine.

A good settlement may be gained by apprenticeship to almost any occupation; thus this privilege was held to be obtained in one case where a female was bound to the wife of a day labourer to learn the art of a housewife. There is, indeed, one exception to this:— no settlement can now be acquired by apprenticeship to the sea service, or to any householder exercising the trade of the seas as a fisherman or otherwise.

The contract must, to give a settlement, be one of *apprenticeship.* No settlement will be given by one of mere *hiring and service.* The distinction between the two may be thus stated:—If the contract has for its object the instruction of the party who is to learn, it is a contract of apprenticeship; but if the principal object be a service to be performed to the master, it is a hiring and service, although the master is also to teach and the servant to learn some particular art or trade.

The binding of an apprentice must take place by deed, duly stamped, &c. But no technical expressions are essential to its validity, provided the parties show clearly that they intend to create the relation of master and apprentice.

Something more than mere apprenticeship is, however, necessary to confer a settlement. The apprentice must, during the term for which he is bound, *inhabit* some parish for forty days, under the indenture, *i. e.* in the character of an apprentice, and in some way or other in furtherance of the objects of the apprenticeship. The inhabitancy is where the apprentice sleeps, and the settlement is gained there, although the service may be in another parish. The forty days need not be consecutive. But when the apprentice resides alternately in two parishes, the settlement is gained where he lodges for the last forty days of the term. And when it is said that the inhabitancy is where the apprentice sleeps, this must be understood of a place where he sleeps under the indenture, or by the direction of his master. If he be allowed, *as a matter of indulgence,* to sleep in another parish than that in which his service takes place, he will acquire no settlement in the former.

Service with a third party during the term of apprenticeship is sufficient, if it be with the master's con-

sent, or with the consent of any person to whom the
master has assigned the indenture.

Indentures may be discharged :—1. By application
of either party to two justices or to the quarter sessions.   2. By death or bankruptcy of the master.   3.
By the apprentice attaining his majority.   4. By consent.

5. *By Hiring and Service.*—The settlement by
hiring and service, which has given rise to more litigation than any other, was founded upon 3 Wm. and
Mary c. 11, and 9 & 10 Wm. 3, c. 30.   The first
of these statutes enacts, that if any unmarried person,
not having child or children, shall be lawfully hired
into any parish or town for one year, such service shall
be adjudged a good settlement, although no notice in
writing be given to the parish officers.

In consequence of the ambiguity attendant upon
the words "such service" in this clause, the 9 & 10
Wm. 3, c. 30, s. 4, provides that no person so hired
shall be judged or deemed to have a good settlement
in any such parish or town, " unless such person shall
continue and abide in the same service for the space of
one whole year."   This does not mean a service entirely
under the same hiring, for if there be a hiring for a
year and a continued service for a year, though not
under the same hiring, it will be sufficient.   Thus a
hiring for half a year, or even for a week, and then a
hiring for a year and a service, part under the other,
would under these acts gain a settlement.   But it is
not of much practical importance to dwell upon these
points ; for this method of gaining a settlement was
prospectively terminated by the New Poor Law Act,

which provided that, after the 14th August, 1834, no settlement shall be acquired by hiring and service or by residence under the same, and no person under any contract of hiring and service not completed on the 14th of August, 1834, shall acquire or demand, or be adjudged to have acquired, any settlement by reason of such hiring and service, or of any residence under the same. The result is, therefore, that no person can now acquire a settlement by hiring and service.

6. *By renting a tenement.*—The method by, and the conditions under, which a settlement by renting a tenement in a parish can be obtained, have varied so frequently since the statutes 13 & 14 Car. 2, c. 12, s. 1, by which it was first established, that it is quite impossible for us to follow it through its modifications. It will probably be sufficient if we go back for a period of nearly forty years. By the 1 Wm. 4, c. 18, it was enacted that, from and after the 30th of March, 1831, no person shall acquire a settlement in any parish or township maintaining its own poor by or by reason of a yearly hiring of a dwelling-house or building, or of land, or of both, as in the said act expressed, unless such house or building or land *shall be actually occupied under such yearly hiring* in the same parish or township *by the person hiring the same* for the term of one whole year at the least, and unless the rent for the same, to the amount of £10 at the least, shall be paid by the person hiring the same. The words in *Italics* are most material, for it has been decided, in reference to them, that no settlement of this kind can now be gained where any portion of the premises in respect of which it is claimed have been under-let by the claimant.

And by the 4 & 5 Wm. 4, c. 76, s. 66 (the New
Poor Law Act), no settlement can be acquired or completed since the 14th of August, 1834, by occupying
a tenement, unless the person occupying the same has
been assessed to the poor-rate, and has paid the same
in respect of such tenement for one year.   Where the
rate is imposed on the tenement (though the name of
the party rated is not mentioned in the rate), and it
is demanded of and paid by the occupier, that is a
sufficient assessment of him.*

7. *By payment of rates.*—This settlement is now
practically the same as the last, with one important
exception.   Although it is necessary, in order to gain
it, that a claimant should have occupied a tenement to
the value of £10, under a yearly hiring, paid parochial
rates and taxes in respect of it, &c., the fact that he
has under-let a portion of it will not (so that he has
himself paid rent to the amount of £10) disqualify him
from claiming a settlement in virtue of the payment of
all parochial rates that have been charged upon him
during his occupancy.   It is necessary, however, in
order to complete his title to a settlement of this kind,
that he should have resided in the parish forty days
after the payment of rates.

8. *By estate.*—Whenever a person acquires an estate
in land (whether it be freehold, copyhold, or lease-
hold) by *descent, devise,*† by *marriage,* or by a gift" i n
consideration of natural love and affection," *what-*

* Where the yearly rent exceeds £10, payment to the extent of £10 will suffice ; but it must in all cases be by the
person renting.
† *i. e.* By a will.

R

ever be its value, and he resides on it, or in the same
parish in which it is situate, for forty days, he gains, and
although he parts with it immediately afterwards, he
retains, a settlement in that parish. But if he obtains
the estate by *purchase*, then, unless the purchase-money
bonâ fide paid for it amounts to £30 or upwards, he will
only ·gain and retain a settlement in respect of his
ownership so long as he actually resides upon and occupies the estate. Immediately he ceases to do so, the
settlement also ceases, and he may be removed (if
chargeable to the poor rate) to the parish of his last
previous settlement.

And with respect to settlements of this kind, whether the estate is gained by descent, devise, marriage,
or gift, or is acquired by purchase, and whatever be
its value, the 4 & 5 Wm. 4, c. 76, s. 68, enacts that
no person shall retain any settlement gained by virtue
of any possession of an estate, or interest in any
parish, for any longer time than such person shall inhabit within ten miles thereof; and in case any person
shall cease to inhabit within such distance, and thereafter become chargeable, such pauper shall be liable to
be removed to the parish wherein, previously to such
inhabitancy, he may have been legally settled ; or in
case he may have, subsequently to such inhabitancy,
gained a legal settlement in some other parish, then to
such other parish. The effect of this section, therefore, is, that if a person once removes more than ten
miles from the parish containing his estate, his settlement in respect of such estate ceases, and he can only
renew it by a fresh residence of forty days in the

parish, while still owner of the property in respect of which he claims.

And it must also be remarked that, although a residence of forty days in the parish is requisite to confer, in virtue of an estate, a settlement which will continue after a person has ceased to reside upon or own it, no man can be removed from his own estate (whatever its value) while he resides upon it.

9. *By serving an office.*—Any person who, before the 14th August, 1834, had resided in a parish for forty days, and had served therein (having been lawfully appointed) any public annual office during one *whole* year, gained thereby a settlement. As the New Poor Law Act prohibited any further settlements being thus acquired after the date we have just named, this head of the law of settlement has now lost much of the little practical importance it ever possessed.

It only remains to add, that a person competent to acquire a settlement by his or her own act (by apprenticeship, hiring and service, renting a tenement, payment of rates, and holding an estate or office) is at any given time settled in the parish where he or she *last* acquired a settlement by any one of these means: a *later*—so long as it lasts—supersedes an *earlier* settlement.

Part II.—Removal.

The law of *settlement* confers upon persons, under the conditions we have just stated, the right to receive relief in the unions which comprise the parishes of their settlement; the law of *removal* authorizes magistrates to remove persons chargeable to the poor rates from the union in which they have become so chargeable to the unions which comprise the parishes where they have obtained a settlement, in order that they may there receive the relief to which they are entitled. Formerly, the two laws were exactly correlative; in other words, a person residing and becoming chargeable in a parish where he was not settled, was, under all circumstances, liable to be removed to a parish in which he was settled. Various statutes have, however, introduced exceptions to this rule, and there are now several classes of persons who cannot be removed from the unions in which they reside, although they have no settlement there. Indeed, since the act of 1865, which reduced to a single year the period of residence requisite to confer the right or privilege of irremovability, the exceptions may now be said to be the rule. So few persons become chargeable within the first twelve months of their residence in a foreign union, that removals have, in fact (as was intended by the framers of the act), been reduced within the narrowest limit.

The most important acts in regard to this subject are the 9 & 10 Vict. c. 66, the 24 & 25 Vict. c. 55, and the 28 & 29 Vict. c. 79. Read together, they enact that no person is to be removed, nor is any warrant to be granted for the removal of any person, from any union in which he has resided for one year next before the application for the warrant; and it is provided that "the residence of a person in any part of a union shall have the same effect in reference to the provisions of the said section [9 & 10 Vict. c. 66, s. 1], as a residence in any parish." * The

* "In the case of any poor person hereinbefore chargeable,

residence must have been continuous. "If there be a break in the residence, the privilege of irremovability ceases. There has been a great deal of discussion as to what will constitute a break of residence; but the result of the case seems to be, that so long as the pauper has the power and intention of returning to the parish, and is absent therefrom voluntarily and for a mere temporary purpose, his residence there will continue, so as to confer irremovability. Thus where the pauper, being out of work, went to his place of settlement to seek for employment, leaving his wife and family at the lodgings where he had previously resided, and was employed for about six weeks by the overseers of his place of settlement, after which he returned to his lodgings and resided there with his family until an order of removal was obtained, it is held, that the circumstances showed an intention of returning on the part of the pauper, and that his absence is no break-of residence. When, however, the absence is under a contract for service, and the party has no intention of returning, unless events over which he has no control occur, as where he only intended to return if he quitted the service, which he had no desire to do, this is a break of residence." *

Imprisonment, whether it be in or out of the union

or hereafter becoming chargeable, in any parish comprised in a union, not being the parish of his settlement, the period of time during which he shall have resided in the parish of the settlement, if in the same union, shall not be excluded in the computation of the time of residence required to render him exempt from removal under the statutes above referred to." 27 & 28 Vict. c. 105, s. 1.

* Steer's Parish Law, by Hodgson, p. 711.

where the pauper has resided for a year, and whether it be upon a criminal charge or for a civil debt, or confinement in a lunatic asylum, does not operate as a break of that residence. But the time during which such person is in prison, or is serving Her Majesty as a soldier, marine, or sailor, or resides as an in-pensioner in Greenwich or Chelsea hospitals, or is confined in a lunatic asylum, or is a patient in a hospital, or during which he receives relief from any parish, or is wholly or in part maintained by any rate or subscription raised in a parish in which he does not reside, not being a *bonâ fide* charitable gift, is, for all purposes, to be excluded from the computation of the time above mentioned.

The following are other cases of irremovability:—

No woman residing in any parish with her husband at the time of his death is to be removed, nor is any warrant to be granted for her removal, from such parish for twelve calendar months next after his death, if she so long continue a widow. When a married woman has been deserted by her husband, and has after her desertion resided for three years in such a manner as would, if she were a widow, render her exempt from removal, she will not be liable to removal from the parish wherein she is resident unless her husband return to cohabit with her. No child under the age of sixteen, whether legitimate or illegitimate, residing in any parish with its father or mother, stepfather or stepmother, or reputed father, is to be removed, nor is any warrant to be granted for its removal, from any parish in any case where such father, &c., may not be lawfully removed from such parish.

Where a child under the age of sixteen years, residing with its surviving parent, is left an orphan, and such parent has at the time of his death acquired an exemption from removal by reason of a continual residence, such orphan will, if not otherwise irremovable, be exempt from removal in like manner and to the same extent as if it had then acquired for itself an exemption from removal by residence. Whenever a person has a wife or children having no other settlement than his own, such wife and children are to be removable whenever he would be removable, and not removable when he would not be removable. A wife cannot be removed from a husband, whether he have a settlement or no. And by the 9 & 10 Vict. c. 66, s. 4, no warrant is to be granted for the removal of any person becoming chargeable in respect of relief made necessary by sickness or accident, unless the justices granting the warrant state therein that they are satisfied that it will produce permanent disability.*

Subject to these exceptions, any persons *coming to reside in any union* in which they are not settled, and *becoming chargeable to the poor rates there,* may be removed by an order or warrant of two justices (granted upon the application of the guardians of such union) to the parish or union where they were last legally settled. The power of removal is thus rendered dependent upon two conditions:—1st. The pauper must have come to what we may call the foreign union *for the purpose of residing there.* Persons who have

* Blindness is a sickness producing permanent disability within this clause. Whether or no lunacy is, is a doubtful point.

not come there with that intention, but are detained
there by sickness, accident, or casualty, and thus
become chargeable to the rates, are not removable.
2nd. Before a person can be removed, he must be in
actual receipt of relief. Persons convicted of felony,
or convicted under the 5 Geo. 4, c. 83, s. 20, of
being idle and disorderly persons, or rogues and
vagabonds, are to be deemed actually chargeable to
the place in which they reside, and removable therefrom.

The removal is to be made to the union comprising
the parish or place where the pauper was last legally
settled. It is to be made by or under the direction
of the guardians of the union to which he has become
chargeable, who may employ any proper person to
remove and deliver him in the union to which he is
removed. The pauper is not to be removed until
notice of the order (with other documents) has been
sent to the guardians of the union to which he is to be
removed, unless they previously, by writing under their
hands, agree to submit to the order ; nor is he to be
removed if they apply for a copy of the depositions
upon which the order is founded, until fourteen days
after the depositions have been sent. And if within
the above twenty-one days, or the further period of
fourteen days, such latter guardians give notice of
their intention to appeal against the order, the pauper
cannot be removed until after the time for prosecuting
the appeal has expired, or if it be duly prosecuted,
until after it has been finally determined.

The pauper is to be delivered at the workhouse of
the union to which he is removed. And it is an

indictable offence to refuse to receive paupers duly removed.

And by the 9 & 10 Vict. c. 66, and the 14 & 15 Vict. c. 105, if any officer of any parish or union, contrary to law, with intent to cause any poor person to become chargeable to any parish to which he was not then chargeable, conveys him out of the parish for which such officer acts, or causes or procures him to be so conveyed, or gives, directly or indirectly, any money, relief, or assistance, or affords or procures to be afforded any facility for such conveyance, or makes any offer or promise, or uses any threat to induce any poor person to depart from such parish, and if, in consequence of such conveyance or departure, any poor person becomes chargeable to any parish to which he was not chargeable, such officer, on conviction before two justices of the county or jurisdiction in which the parish from which such poor person is removed is situate, is to forfeit for every such offence a sum not exceeding £5, nor less than 40s. The penalty is to be applied in aid of the poor rates of the parish to which the poor person becomes chargeable.

Every person returning in a state of vagrancy, and becoming chargeable to a union, parish, &c., from which he has been lawfully removed, unless he produce a certificate acknowledging him to be settled in some other union or parish, is to be deemed an idle and disorderly person, and may be punished accordingly.

We have said that an order of removal must be made by two justices, acting in and for the county in which the parish to which the pauper is chargeable is situate, or by a metropolitan police magistrate. It must be made on complaint of the guardians of the union seeking to remove; and must be made upon proof of the circumstances which we have seen are necessary to render a pauper removable. Notice of the pauper having become chargeable, a copy of the order of removal, and a statement of the grounds of removal, including the settlement or settlements relied upon in support thereof, are then to be sent by the guardians of the union obtaining such order, to the guardians of the union to which it is directed. And the latter, on giving notice of their intention within twenty-one days, may appeal against the order of removal to the quarter sessions of the county, division, or riding, or of the municipal borough, in which is situate the parish, township, or place from which the pauper is removed. The sessions may either confirm or rescind the order. The general statement of the law and procedure in respect to removal may suffice in a work of this popular character. Any further information upon this intricate subject must be sought in those purely professional works where alone it can be usefully conveyed.

It only remains to notice, in connection with this part of our subject, the principal provisions of the laws regulating the removal of Scotch, Irish, &c., paupers. Under the 8 & 9 Vict. c. 117, s. 1, if any person born in Scotland or Ireland or the Isle of Man, Scilly, Jersey, or Guernsey, and not settled in England, becomes chargeable to any parish in England by reason of relief given to him or herself, or to his wife, or any legitimate or bastard child, such person, his wife, and any child so chargeable, are liable to be

removed respectively to Scotland, Ireland, &c., and if
the guardians of such parish or of any union in which
it is comprised, or, where there are no such guardians,
the overseers of such parish, complain to two or more
justices in petty sessions * assembled, or to a stipendiary magistrate, or to a Metropolitan police magistrate, they or he may, if such person do not attend
voluntarily, summon him to come before two justices
at a time and place named in the summons, who may
hear and examine into the complaint; and if it appear
that such person is liable to be removed † as aforesaid,
and if they see fit, they may issue a warrant under
their hands and seals, to remove him forthwith at the
expense of such union or parish.

CHAPTER. XXXIII.

OF PARISH APPRENTICES.

THE binding of parish apprentices is now regulated
by the consolidated order of the Poor Law board of
the 24th July, 1847, which contains the following
regulations :—

No child under the age of nine years, and no child
(other than a deaf and dumb child) who cannot read
and write his own name, shall be bound apprentice by
the guardians.

No child shall be so bound to a person who is not

* 25 & 26 Vict. c. 113, s. 1.

† The grounds of *irremovability* applicable to English paupers, are equally so where the persons proposed to be removed
are Scotch, Irish, &c.

a housekeeper, or assessed to the poor rate in his own name, or who is a journeyman or person not carrying on trade or business on his own account, or who is under the age of twenty-one; or who is a married woman.

No premium other than clothing for the apprentice shall be given upon the binding of any person above the age of sixteen years, unless such person be suffering from some permanent bodily infirmity, such as may render him unfit for certain trades or sorts of work.

When any premium is given, it shall in part consist of clothes, supplied to the apprentice at the commencement of the binding, and part in money, one moiety whereof shall be paid to the master at the binding, and the residue at the termination of the first year of the binding.

No apprentice shall be bound by the guardians for more than eight years.

No person above fourteen years shall be so bound without his consent. And no child under the age of sixteen years shall be so bound without the consent of the father of such child, or if the father be dead, or disqualified to give such consent as hereinafter provided, or, if such child be a bastard, without the consent of the mother, if living, of such child. Provided, that where such parent is transported beyond the seas, or is in custody of the law, having been convicted of some felony, or, for the space of six calendar months before the time of executing the indenture, has deserted such child, or for such space of time has been in the service of Her Majesty in any place out of the kingdom, such parent, shall be deemed to be disqualified as hereinbefore stated ; and if it be the mother, no such consent shall be required.

No child shall be bound to a master whose place of business whereat the child is to work and live is more than thirty miles from the place at which the child is residing at the time of the proposed binding, or at the time of his being sent on trial to such master ; unless in any particular case the commissioners shall, on application to them, otherwise permit.

The order then requires the guardians, when the child is under fourteen years of age, to assure themselves, by a proper medical certificate, that he is, in point of health and strength, fit for the trade to which it is proposed to bind him. This point having been ascertained, the guardians are to direct that the child and the proposed master, or some person on his behalf, and, in case the child be under the age of sixteen, that the parent or person in whose custody such child shall be then living, shall attend some meeting of the board to be then appointed.

At such meeting, if such parties appear, the guardians shall examine into the circumstances of the case ; and if, after making all due inquiries and hearing the objections (if any be made) on the part of the relatives or friends of such child, they deem it proper that the binding be effected, they may forthwith cause the indenture to be prepared, and, if the master be present, to be executed; but if he be not present, they shall cause the same to be transmitted to him for execution ; and when executed by him and returned to the guardians, the same shall be executed by the latter, and signed by the child.

If the proposed master reside out of the union, but in some other union or parish under a board of guardians, the guardians shall, before proceeding to effect the binding, communicate in writing the proposal to the guardians of such other union or parish, and request to be informed whether such binding is open to any objection; and if no objection be reported by such guardians within the space of one calendar month, or if the objection does not appear to the guardians proposing to bind the child to be sufficient to prevent the binding, the same may be proceeded with, and when the indenture shall have been executed, the clerk of the guardians who executed the same shall send notice thereof in writing to the guardians of the union or parish wherein the said apprentice is to reside.

Other articles prescribe the mode of executing the indenture and the stipulations to be inserted in it, at too great a length, however, to be given here. One of the most important is, that the master shall covenant, under a penalty, not to assign or cancel the indenture without the consent of the guardians under their common seal previously obtained, and to pay to the said guardians all costs and expenses that they may incur in consequence of the said apprentice not being supplied with medical or surgical assistance by the master, in case the same shall at any time be requisite.

The indenture shall be made subject to the following provisoes :—

1. That if the master take the benefit of any act for the relief of insolvent debtors, or be discharged

under any such act, such indenture shall forthwith become of no further force or effect.

2. That if, on a conviction for a breach of any one of the aforesaid covenants and conditions before a justice of the peace, the guardians who may be parties to the said indenture declare by a resolution that the indenture is determined, and transmit a copy of such resolution under the hand of their clerk, by the post or otherwise, to the said master, such indenture shall, except in respect of all rights and liabilities then accrued, forthwith become of no further force and effect.

Nothing contained in this order is to apply to the apprenticing of poor children to the sea service.*

It will be observed, that under the above order a covenant is to be inserted in every indenture of the description to which we are now referring, that the apprentice is not to be assigned or transferred to a new master without the consent of the guardians. The consent of two justices is also requisite under the 56 Geo. 3, c. 139, which provides, that assigning a parish apprentice or discharging him from service without such consent, is an offence for which a penalty not exceeding £10 may be inflicted.

---

* The apprenticing children to the sea-service by overseers or guardians is now regulated by the 7 & 8 Vict. c. 112, ss. 32–43, and the 17 & 18 Vict. c. 104, ss. 141–5.

Woodfall and Kinder, Printers, Milford Lane, Strand, London, W.C.

For EU product safety concerns, contact us at Calle de José Abascal, 56–1°, 28003 Madrid, Spain or eugpsr@cambridge.org.

www.ingramcontent.com/pod-product-compliance
Ingram Content Group UK Ltd.
Pitfield, Milton Keynes, MK11 3LW, UK
UKHW010342140625
459647UK00010B/778